A Civil Dissolution:

The Best Solution to America's Irreconcilable Ideological Conflict

Laurie Thomas Vass

The Great American Business & Economics Press
GABBY Press

Copyright © 2023. The Great American Business & Economics Press. GABBY Press.

All rights reserved under Title 17, U.S. Code, International and Pan-American copyright Conventions.

No part of this work may be reproduced or transmitted in any form or by any means, electronic or mechanical, including photocopying, scanning, recording or duplication by any information storage or retrieval system without prior written permission from the author(s) and publisher(s), except for the inclusion of brief quotations with attribution in a review or report. Requests for reproductions or related information should be addressed to the author c/o Great American Business & Economics Press, 620 Kingfisher Lane SW, Sunset Beach, N. C. 28468.

Printed in the United States of America.

Revised December 2023.

Table of Contents: A Civil Dissolution: The Best Solution to America's Irreconcilable Ideological Conflict

Introduction. Obama's America.	5
Chapter 1. The Logic of National Divorce and Civil Dissolution.	16
Chapter 2. The End of the American Rule of Law.	44
Chapter 3. Starting America Over At 1776.	64
Chapter 4. Replacing Madison's Rules of Civil Procedure In Order to Enshrine Liberty as the Public Purpose.	93
Chapter 5. New Constitutional Rules for Economic Growth and Financial Stability.	121
Chapter 6. Establishing Constitutional Public Purpose of National Economic Sovereignty.	155
Chapter 7. The Entrepreneurial Capitalist Constitutional Public Purpose.	201
Chapter 8. Towards An Absolute National Divorce and Permanent Civil Dissolution.	233
Bibliography.	255

Introduction: Obama's America.

In the 2008 U. S. presidential election, decent, good-hearted, Americans elected a smiling, genial Black person, who promised to heal the nation's racial wounds.

What those citizens got instead of healing was eight years of racial violence, the weaponisation of the agencies of government against political opponents, and the Marxist rhetoric of class war.

Obama deployed a rhetorical charade during the 2008 campaign to convince White voters that he was a new transformational candidate, not like traditional Democrat Black nationalist candidates, who exclusively promote a Black Marxist ideology.

Obama's promise of racial harmony was simply a rhetorical ruse to obtain votes from White voters.

As explained by Noam Scheiber in his May 30, 2004, New Republic article:

"Whereas many working-class voters are wary of African American candidates, whom they think will promote Black interests at the expense of their own, [working class] they simply don't see Obama in these terms. This allows him to appeal to White voters on traditional Democratic issues like jobs, health care, and education—just like a White candidate would."

"There's not a Black America and White America," said Obama, at the 2004, Democrat Convention, "there's the United States of America."

The rhetorical technique used by Obama was a powerful propaganda tool to promote Obama's ideology of new world order Marxism.

In the charade, Obama used the ethical norms of individualist behavior for the original American natural rights culture, and connected the civil values declared in Jefferson's Declaration with the collectivist group identity values and experiences of Black Lives Matter (BLM.).

When White voters heard Obama's message of racial harmony, they were relieved of their guilt of constitutional White privilege, and subsequently voted for Obama.

After Obama obtained the White vote, and was elected, he jettisoned the racial harmony charade, and embarked on an 8 year mission of transforming America into a global socialist state, using European social class income equality as his model.

Throughout his tenure, Obama continually invoked the symbols of racism and slavery, in a three step political strategy, to transform America into a global socialist state.

The first part of his strategy was to create race hatred between Whites and Blacks in order to attract converts who began to hate America, and who had a heightened sense of grievance about Madison's compromises to embed the legality of slavery into the Constitution.

The second part of Obama's strategy was to promise the aggrieved and downtrodden Black citizens that he, and the Democrats, would remedy their grievances against the right-wing White supremacists forces that were oppressing them.

The final part of Obama's strategy was to use tax-funded welfare payments to hook the downtrodden into a life of dependency on the socialist government.

Obama understood that once the citizens become servile, they would lose their capacity for objective, independent rational decision-making, the bedrock citizen requirement in a natural rights republic.

The increase in welfare payments had the economic and labor market effect of reducing the incentive for millions of working class citizens to work in the private economy.

Obama knew that his hardest job in the 3-step conversion process was the very first part of making both Black and White lower class citizens hate America.

As he had been taught by his socialist teacher, Saul Alinsky, Obama knew that once citizens give up their rights in exchange for government welfare, the socialists would be able control the citizens for life by controlling the ideology of socialist class hatred.

Once Obama began using the weapons of racism and class to divide America, he could never stop ginning up hatred between the races.

Obama weaponized the Department of Justice to target his political opponents for political oppression and used a two-tier justice system to absolve his Democrat collaborators of criminal investigation.

Obama's rhetoric of hate created an environment of violence, and as the ideological rhetoric went up, so did the violence caused by the leftist propaganda.

With the transformation of the Democrat Party into a global socialist party, and not the historic party that represented common citizens, Madison's constitutional system of checks and balances between social classes was rendered inoperative.

Madison's constitutional framework of checks and balances was based upon the European government model of social class conflict between the ruling class and common citizens.

In Madison's political system, the agencies of government were intended to check the populist sentiments of the majority that would use their majority votes to deprive the ruling class of property rights.

As long as the United States had two competing political parties, who represented social class financial interests, Madison's representative republic offered political stability.

In the 2012 presidential election campaign, Obama jettisoned the prior Democrat Party social class interests of working class citizens in favor of an overtly class and race war ideology of socialism.

The transformation of the Democrat Party from a social class based political party to an ideological class and race war political party is a permanent change in American politics.

The Democrat Marxists will never go back to being a social class based political party that represented the commercial interests of common citizens.

Even if the Republican Party happened to win an election in the future, the Democrat Marxists will continue their quest to undermine the American political system in order to achieve permanent authoritarian power.

The Republican Party continues to function under the old two-class competition framework of Madison, and has not adopted an ideological defense of individual liberty that confronts the Democrat Marxist vision of collectivism.

Madison's compromises on slavery at the writing of the Constitution of 1787 will never end as useful propaganda tool for the Marxist Democrats.

As Obama said, in March 2008, Madison's constitution was irrevocably flawed:

"The document they produced was eventually signed but ultimately unfinished. It was stained by this nation's original sin of slavery, a question that divided the colonies and brought the convention to a stalemate until the founders chose to allow the slave trade to continue for at least twenty more years, and to leave any final resolution to future generations."

We agree with Obama that Madison's constitution is flawed, but not simply because it left the issue of slavery to be solved on the field of battle.

Madison's constitution concentrated political power in the hands of the natural aristocracy, and failed to state, in the Preamble, that protection of liberty was the main goal of the national government.

The concentration of power that was reserved to the ruling class, under Madison's checks and balances, was obtained by the Democrats in the stolen election of 2020.

In the two party political system created by Madison, in the period of time after 2012, common citizens no longer had their own political party (faction) to represent their class interests.

In the absence of their own political party, common citizens did not have the constitutional power to protect their natural rights from the Marxist onslaught.

The future that is in store for White citizens in America, as long as the Black Marxists are able to invoke the image of slavery, is increasing violence and a loss of individual freedom.

The prosecution of President Trump by the Democrat Black Marxist DAs. in New York and Georgia, and the prosecution by Jack Smith, in the January 6, 2021, incident is only a precursor of what the Black Marxists have in mind for the rest of White American society.

The prosecution of Trump is ideologically based in order to eliminate a political opponent. From the perspective of the Marxist Democrats, all of Trump's supporters are also enemies of the state, equally warranted to be targeted for political reprisal.

As the time pattern of violent riots and police shootings show, Obama, and the Democrats, are able to turn on and off the violence whenever Soros tells them to.

This pattern of controlled political violence is a very effective tool of the Soros strategy to eradicate the American system of the rule of law and national sovereignty, in order to replace United States national sovereignty with a one-world authoritarian government.

In global socialism, a very small set of banking and corporate elites make all of the political decisions, on behalf of all citizens.

Socialists use a type of logic called cultural relativism, which suggests that all cultures are morally equal.

In the deployment of this logic, America's flawed origin of slavery makes the nation morally equivalent to every other oppressive culture.

For example, in the case of Hamas attacking Israel in 2023, BLM issued a statement of support and solidarity with the Muslims who conducted the attack.

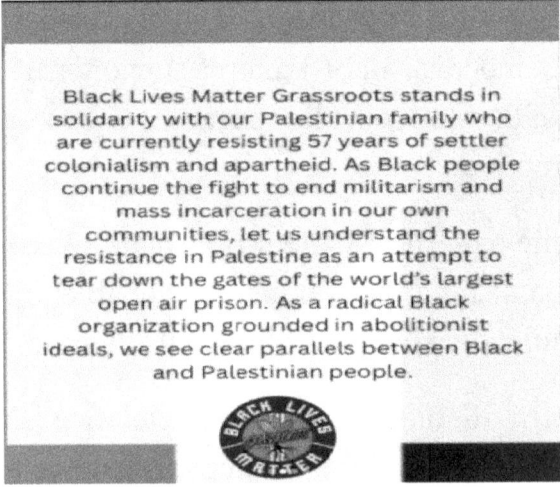

In the logic of Marxist cultural relativism, the oppression of Black people in America is equivalent to the oppression of Muslim Hamas terrorists because they both share a history of oppression by White people.

America, as a society, according to BLM, is equivalent to the racism and oppression of Israel against the Palestinians in promoting the evil of slavery.

In addition to multi-cultural relativism, the socialists use a unique form of propaganda to promote their religion called critical legal studies (CLS).

The ostensible goal of CLS is to use the two-tiered justice system to enforce their version of "fairness" in the distribution of incomes.

Under the logic of Democrat Marxism, citizens are born into a state of permanent subjugation to an alien White authority, precisely the opposite of Jefferson's principle that all men are born equal and subject to no laws that, they themselves, do not give to themselves.

On every single principle of a natural rights republic, the socialists have an alien, subversive view of America.

The moral and ideological differences between Marxist Democrats and natural rights conservatives are irreconcilable.

This book explains why the philosophical differences between the two groups of voters are irreconcilable and presents the argument that a civil dissolution of the nation into socialist slave and liberty free states is the best possible strategy to resolve the ideological conflict.

The only peaceful, nonviolent, solution to resolve the differences between Democrat Marxists and natural rights conservatives is to allow citizens in each state to vote on civil dissolution.

We propose providing citizens with three options about the future of the Nation:

1. Vote to leave the existing nation to form a new nation that is true to the original principles of government expressed by Jefferson in 1776.
2. Vote to leave the existing nation to form a new Socialist States of America.
3. Vote to remain under Madison's constitutional rules in a centralized authoritarian government that is a component of a new global one world order.

Our book offers the logic of an absolute divorce and permanent civil dissolution for natural rights conservatives to form the Democratic Republic of American States.

Chapter 1. The Logic of National Divorce and Civil Dissolution.

American conservative citizens are now in a state of war declared by the Democrat Marxist national government to rid society of enemies deemed white terrorists..

It is an ideological war over the mission of the national government.

The war was declared by the Marxist Democrats after Trump won the 2016 election.

It is a one-sided war, with one side on the field of battle, using the resources of the deep state to target and eliminate political enemies. The Democrat Marxists possess a coherent ideology based upon class and race grievances.

The other side of the war is disorganized and unfunded, and has yet to place an army on the field of battle. Conservatives do not have a middle class ideology to direct their forces and has no political party to lead them into battle.

Madison's constitution was based upon a two-class commercial competition between the natural aristocracy and common citizens.

Madison's rules were designed to ameliorate economic conflicts, not ideological conflicts.

In Madison's conception of government, the apparatus of government is a neutral guardian between the two competing social class interests that his constitutional separation of power was designed to check and balance.

Madison assumed that his political rules would provide social stability, as long as the levers of centralized power remained in the hands of the virtuous natural aristocracy.

In other words, Madison's constitution is a set of non-ideological rules of civil procedure for making decisions, and is incapable of resolving ideological conflicts that are not about property rights.

We agree with the analysis of Emerald Robinson that, after the stolen election of November 2020, the Democrat Marxists have seized power permanently.

In her recent Substack article, "The Biden Regime Goes Rogue," Emerald Robinson begins by asking:

"Who is going to stop them?"

Her point is that Madison's constitution has no provisions to stop the consolidated, centralized police power of the state. The deep state has become a tyrannical Leviathan.

Robinson points out in her article that,

"Consider the possibility that Democrats are seizing power permanently. They have the secret police and the corporate media and the federal government and the universities and Hollywood and Silicon Valley and Big Pharma and Wall Street on their side. They've already crossed the line — as the raid on Trump's mansion made clear to most Americans — so why [should Merrick Garland] stop now?"

What is now a permanent feature of American politics is the entrance of Marxist ideology as the organizing force for part of the American population that is attracted to socialism.

Beginning in early 2017, just after the election of Trump, socialist writers began imagining how Marxist ideology would work, for them, as a strategy for obtaining permanent power, and imposing a socialist state.

Our review of their publications and perspective of conservatives as racist enemies of the state is intended to contrast their coherent ideology of Marxism with the absence of an alternative ideology of individual liberty by natural rights conservatives.

One of the left's most detailed books about obtaining permanent power was "It's Time to Fight Dirty: How Democrats Can Build a Lasting Majority in American Politics," (2018), by political scientist David Faris.

Faris is an Associate Professor of Political Science at Roosevelt University in downtown Chicago.

Faris details how Trump's administration can be overthrown through a process of undermining the integrity of the election system, beginning in the election of 2020.

In his book, Faris argues that Democrats should stop worrying about the legality and morality of their election and vote counting strategies.

He suggests that a better idea for Marxists is to undermine the legality of the elections system by "fighting dirty." His recommendations were implemented in the election of 2020.

Faris writes,

"You cannot win, in the long term, on a policy or messaging fight on a playing field that is tilted hopelessly against you…The book was inspired by two things. Total depression on election night [Trump victory] and then thinking about what it would take for Democrats to recapture power given these structural obstacles."

The structural obstacles he cites are election outcomes based upon majority rule.

Faris goes on to recommend a slew of ways Democrats can "fight dirty," by which he means subverting the rules of American politics by implementing mail-in ballots, ballot harvesting and fraud in counting the votes.

In their review of the Faris book, The New York Times Book Review noted,

"In [this] short, bracing book, David Faris ... argues that Democrats should immediately use every lever they have to gum up the works in Washington, to ensure they win full control of government in 2020."

Two months after Trumps inauguration, another leftist wrote about

"a declaration of independence from Trump's America."

In his New Republic article, Kevin Baker writes,

"What I mean is that it's time for blue states and cities to effectively abandon the American national enterprise, as it is currently constituted. Call it the New Federalism. Or Virtual Secession. Or Conscious Uncoupling—though that's already been used. Or maybe Bluexit…We'll turn Blue America into a world-class incubator for progressive programs and policies, a laboratory for a guaranteed income and a high-speed public rail system and free public universities. We'll focus on getting our own house in order, while yours [natural rights conservatives] falls into disrepair and ruin. Since you [MAGA Trump voters} will not hear our words, we will need to convince you by our actions. We will need to run our states and our cities so well, in such an effective and enlightened manner, that we can make you understand all over again what every page of our history should already tell you. Through our own example, we must win you over, American by American, town by town, state by state, until we are once more in a position to mitigate all of the foolish, cruel, and wasteful things you [Trump] are about to inflict on the rest of us, and to move forward once again, as American states united."

His point is that, after the Marxist gain unchallenged power, in 2020, the nation can,

"move forward once again, as American states united," under the banner of global Marxism.

Ezra Klein, writing in Vox, in his article, The Rigging of American Politics, (2018), makes many of the same points as Faris, about the need for Democrats to subvert the integrity of the election system.

Klein writes,

"If there is a threat to American unity, it rests not in the specific concerns of Virginians or Alaskans, but in the growing enmity between Democrats and Republicans. A central problem in any free political system is how to ensure a balanced competition. The problem in our system is that what we have balanced is no longer what's competing."

By rigging the election system, Klein hopes to obtain a unified socialist state, run by Democrat Party elites, who make all decisions, in order to dominate and rule conservatives.

In her recent Nation article, "Should the United States Stay United?" Jessica Suriano makes the case that Trump voters should be controlled by the Marxist elite.

Suriano applies Marxist two-class conflict to argue that there are two incompatible Americas.

She writes,

"The United States has never been an equal, peaceful, or functional nation, despite what the history textbooks say. It was built from genocide, slavery, and stolen land. This year, the Black Lives Matter protests and the abolition movement, coupled with a pandemic that preys most on people consistently excluded from the broken health care system, demonstrate the lie of our "more perfect union" even more."

We agree with Suriano that, after the election of 2020, there are two cultures that share no moral values in common. In other words, there is no logical basis for maintaining a national government because no values are held on common on the mission of the nation.

Jeet Heer, in his article, The Republican Party, Not Trump, Is the Real Threat to American Democracy, suggests that the Republican transgressions are so bad, that the Republican Party must be punished.

He states,

"The disease is localized within the Republican Party. Which is why, if indeed American democracy is in a death loop, any solution must not focus solely on ousting Trump, but on punishing and reforming the GOP...Time and again, the Republican-controlled Congress has ignored, defended, or outright enabled Trump's authoritarian excesses."

In the socialist perspective, the citation to the Republican Party is a direct reference to Trump voters.

Chauncey DeVega, a Marxist author at Salon, summarizes the left's opinion of Trump voters as enemies of the state.

He writes,

"The post-civil rights era Republican Party is hostile to the very idea of (multiracial) democracy. Today's Republican Party and broader conservative movement is racist, sexist and authoritarian."

In other words, if Trump voters were more rational, like socialists, Trump voters would not continue to support Trump.

DeVega cites the socialist professor, Cas Mudde, an authority on the racism and totalitarian characteristics of Trump voters.

Mudde is correct when he describes the essential ingredient of shared cultural values as the glue that holds citizens in a democracy together. His point is that the Republican version of the founding of America is false, in 1776, and that his narrative of the racist founding principles of America, in 1787, is correct.

Mudde states,

"Democracy is prefaced on some shared reality and a basic consensus about the truth. Trumpers and other members of the right-wing have rejected that premise. Without such a common understanding, how is it possible to engage in basic decision-making about politics and society? This question of "alternate realities" is about much more than people who do not care about the truth. I believe that most people on the radical right actually think that they are basing their arguments on the facts. Authoritarians use psychological projection to maintain power and control."

In the socialist version of the truth, the Democrat's Russian-Trump conspiracy is the truth. The goal of the socialist projection is to convince socialist voters of the truth of the Russian-Trump conspiracy.

Mudde states,

"In the United States that language has a very racialized connotation. White people hear "white people" when you say "hard-working Americans." Whereas many minorities will think, "Oh, you said 'hard-working Americans.' You're talking to white people…Working class" is another example. It is amazing how in the U.S. "working class" is used to mean the white working class."

Socialist activist Michael Moore has said that white men who voted for Donald Trump in 2016 are, quite simply, bad people. They are, he argued, downright dangerous -- at least for minorities.

Moore states,

"I refuse to say because we elected Obama that suddenly means everything is ok. White people have not changed. Two-thirds of all white guys voted for Trump. That means anytime you see three white guys walking at you, down the street towards you, two of them voted for Trump."

Derek Thompson, in Who Are Donald Trump's Supporters, Really? explains that Trump voters are racists who want Trump to implement white nationalist policies.

He writes,

"Trump has clearly played on fears of non-white outsiders, by likening Mexican immigrants to rapists, promising to deport illegal immigrants and to build a wall between the U.S. and its neighbors, pledging to keep Muslims out of the country during the Syrian diaspora, and playing coy with his relationship with the KKK."

Chauncey DeVega, in his Salon article, "Yes, Trump will leave office — but his seditious secession movement isn't going away," suggests that a civil war, after Trump leaves office, is necessary to purge racism from the new Marxist nation,

DeVega writes,

"Today's Republican Party is the country's largest white supremacist and white identity organization. Donald Trump is its leader and champion. Despite all of the polite talk of how Trump's and 74 million votes in the 2020 election are the result of "economic anxiety" or "status anxiety," social scientists have repeatedly shown that racism, racial resentment and white supremacist views are the key determinants driving Donald Trump's support…Their psychological, emotional and financial investment in white supremacy is too great to give up. To maintain it, Republicans and Trumpists are willing to risk destroying the nation. Their desperate allegiance to the lost cause of Donald Trump's presidency is proof. [of their moral depravity]."

DeVega uses psychological projection of the Democrat's civil war to explain the Democrat's impeachment strategy.

He writes,

"In a failing democracy such as the United States in the Age of Trump, projection as political strategy is another way of attacking truth, the bedrock of democracy."

DeVega accurately describes the essential ingredient of the rule of law in holding a government together.

He states,

"When Trump and his agents protest that he is the target of a "coup" or that his adversaries are "corrupt" or "violating the Constitution," this is a way of clouding the public discourse by making reality and the rule of law meaningless. The ultimate goal for an authoritarian like Trump is to hollow out the rule of law so that it can only be used in his service and against his political enemies."

DeVega writes,

"Donald Trump publicly colluded with a foreign power to help steal the 2016 presidential election for him and in response the American people are largely mute and passive. By all reasonable criteria, Trump has shown himself to be an illegitimate president…Trump supporters do not live in the same shared reality as Democrats… Victory over Trump will demand day-to-day acts of civil disobedience. Such acts of resistance and defiance will be crucial if Donald Trump wins re-election in 2020, an outcome that seems increasingly likely."

Carl Bernstein explained that Mueller's report "documented" the conspiracy between Putin and Trump.

He states,

"Preliminary conclusions from the Mueller Report indicate that Donald Trump helped Russia to "destabilize the United States. Donald Trump is likely a Russian asset. for today's Republican Party and conservative movement, aiding and abetting treasonous and traitorous behavior is just a practical tool used to advance their destructive political revolution."

John Halpin, in his article, The Politics of Definition, explains how polarization and projection can be used to implement a socialist regime.

He states,

"We (socialists) need a new strategy of transformation for today's progressive movement. We must pursue an agenda built on a platform of broadly shared economic opportunity and a clear stand on the side of middle- and working-class families."

In Sean Wilentz's new book, No Property in Man, he cites Calhoun's opinion about two Americas, that is a reflection of Suriano's argument of two Americas.

Wilentz writes,

" Calhoun became convinced that "what they call a Nation" was a sham. He knew that the North and South had become two essentially different societies. On the eve of his death in 1850, he said that "it is difficult to see how two peoples so different and hostile can exist together in one common Union."

This same left-wing ideology of two social groups fits into their concept that the conservatives must be dominated and controlled by the Marxist elites

Robin Wright, in her New Yorker article in September 2020, "Is America a Myth? describes the left's logic in seeking permanent power.

She writes,

"The idea that America has a shared past going back into the colonial period is a myth," Colin Woodard, the author of "Union: The Struggle to Forge the Story of United States Nationhood," told me. "We are very different Americas, each with different origin stories and value sets, many of which are incompatible. They led to a Civil War in the past and are a potentially incendiary force in the future."

She deploys leftist logic to argue that the only solution for Marxists is to impose their socialist values on the entire nation, after the war ends.

She writes,

"The American promise has not delivered for many Blacks, Jews, Latinos, Asian-Americans, myriad immigrant groups, and even some whites as well. Hate crimes—acts of violence against people or property based on race, religion, disability, sexual orientation, ethnicity, or gender identity—are a growing problem."

In his new book, "Break It Up: Secession, Division, and the Secret History of America's Imperfect Union," Richard Kreitner fantasizes about "crushing" the Trump voters.

Kreitner explains,

"We're trying to make this country something it has never been, [Marxist Utopia] and they natural rights conservatives] want no part of it. I want to defeat them, I want to crush them, but I think if you look at the country that we have, I just don't know if that's going to be possible. So if it's not going to be possible to make this country something it's never been, maybe we need to start a new one."

In order to make his case about the origins of racist America, Kreitner is forced to mischaracterize the American Revolution as a civil war against the British.

Suriano cites Krietner's new book to explain,

"Kreitner rightly sees the Continental Congress, formed in 1774, as a "spontaneous response to an emergency," not born from widely felt national bonds. Like other recent historians, he depicts the War of Independence as being as much a "civil war"—colonist against colonist."

Ezra Klein cites the new book by David French, "Divided We Fall: America's Secession Threat and How to Restore Our Nation," as the moral justification of the Democrat Marxist quest for permanent power.

Klein writes,

"You open the book with this really ominous line, "It's time for Americans to wake up to a fundamental reality: the continued unity of the United States of America cannot be guaranteed…I see an election coming [2020] that has the possibility to end in a scenario where one side [MAGA] will not accept the legitimacy of the outcome and there's not really going to be a way to resolve that. We don't really have a way to resolve it now."

Klein is correct that there is no way to resolve the ideological conflict, under Madison's constitution because

Madison's constitution is about conflict between two social classes, based on protecting ruling class property rights, not about ideological conflicts between individualism and collectivism.

After the stolen election of 2020, the centralized levers of power given by Madison to the natural aristocracy to protect property rights are now in the hands of the Marxist Democrats, and they seek permanent power.

In his moral arrogance, Klein psychologically projects onto conservatives his fear that Trump voters will not accept the "legitimacy" of the stolen 2020 election.

The only way for Klein to resolve the issue of legitimacy is to compel Trump voters to accept the results through the police force of the deep state.

We extend Zack Beauchamp's article, "The Constitution Was Not Built For This," to explain that the ideological polarization in America will lead either to a non-violent civil disunion or a violent civil war between MAGA Trump voters and Marxist Democrats.

We argue that Beauchamp, a socialist writer for Vox, is correct that Madison's Constitution of 1787, was not built to resolve the growing ideological polarization between socialists and natural rights conservatives over the nation's mission and purpose.

Beauchamp writes,

"Republicans' in the House who did not vote against Trump's impeachment reveals a broken system — and a democracy at real risk of failure. … the GOP's willingness to back the president to the hilt, in spite of clear and obvious evidence of abuses of power, speaks to an urgent threat to American democracy: Our constitutional system is ill-equipped to withstand extreme polarization."

Beauchamp writes,

"Under conditions of extreme polarization, the two camps start to see the other side as not merely a political opponent, but an existential threat to the American way of life."

For Beauchamp, the impeachment of Trump is simply a necessary first step in removing the voting rights of 75 million Trump conservatives, in order to make progress to a hoped-for one-party socialist tyranny.

His argument is that Republicans in the House, who did not support the left's drive for Trump's impeachment, are intolerant and are contributing to the inevitable disunion of the Nation.

We argue that socialists promote class conflict and racial polarization as a strategy to overthrow the government in order to replace the current government with their version of global Marxism,

In the training videos for the new 88,000 IRS police agents, the new agents are required to use lethal force against innocent citizens.

In one training video, the IRS agents are shown breaking into a middle class suburban home, in swat team formation, with AR-15s drawn and aimed at an imaginary citizen.

From that point in the video, imagine that the IRS agents are successful in killing the innocent citizen. The citizen is innocent, because in the Former United States of America, [FUSA] a citizen is innocent, until proven guilty.

Except in this video, the citizen was killed by the IRS agents.

In the psychology of Marxism, the conservative citizen is guilty, before the fact, of being a racist White American terrorist threat, and the IRS agents are justified in the use of lethal force in eliminating a non-Marxist.

Cristina Laila, in her August 16, 2022 Gateway Pundit article on the FBI report "Domestic Violent Extremists," notes that,

"The DHS told its agents that Americans who discuss topics such as "government overreach" and "election fraud" are a threat."

Laila could have added that the citizens who question the government are a threat to the promotion of Marxism, not a threat to public health and safety.

C. Bradley Thompson asks:

"What type of person is attracted to Marxism?"

In his article, "Why Marxism—Evil Laid Bare," Thompson writes,

"The better question here is: What *kind* of person is attracted to Marxism? The best scholarship now tells us that between 1917 and 1989 approximately 100 million people were murdered by various Marxist regimes, and millions more were tortured, starved, exiled, enslaved, and sent to concentration camps. Collectivization, one-party rule, man-made famine, secret police, arrests, propaganda, censorship, ethnic cleansing, purges, show trials, reeducation camps, gulags, firing squads, and killing fields—all these defined life under communism. Nothing in the long span of human history comes close to the tyranny, terror, and mass genocide caused by Marxism in power—*nothing*."

As we noted above, in the Introduction, after the two Black Democrat Marxist DAs, and Jack Smith, get finished persecuting Trump, this same treatment of Trump MAGA supporters is what the Marxists have in mind for conservatives.

The American Democrat Marxists are no different than any other Marxists in history. They all are united in a common ideology that a future Marxist utopia justifies the elimination of their enemies.

Michael Anton, in his new book, "The Stakes: America at the Point of No Return," suggests,

"Then there is the unpleasant fact that Blue America [Democrat Marxists] wants to rule Red in a way that the latter does not want to rule Blue. To borrow from Machiavelli, in the present-day United States, these two diverse humors are found, which arises from this: that the Blues desire to command and oppress the Reds, while the Reds wish to be neither commanded nor oppressed."

The reason for the disparity in allegiance to authoritarianism is that Marxist Democrats have a coherent ideology in obtaining their political goals of permanent power.

Republicans, Trump MAGA voters, and natural rights conservatives do not have a competing ideology because their vision of America is stuck in the past on Madison's two class political model of competition about financial interests.

The fundamental difference cited by Anton, between Marxists and conservatives is the legitimacy of government authority based upon Locke's principle that no one may rule another without his consent.

Marxists do not believe in this principle of consent of the governed, and substitute their allegiance to the future utopian state as the justification for eliminating dissent.

In his recent book, "America's Revolutionary Mind: A Moral History of the American Revolution and the Declaration that Defined It," C. Bradley Thompson explains the Lockean logic of the new nation of 1776.

He writes,

"The new [nation's] moral history begins with certain assumptions about human nature;

- first, that individuals are the primary unit of moral value;
- second, that human nature is knowable and sometimes predictable,
- third, that man's faculty of reason can know cause-and-effect relationships in nature and human nature;
- fourth, that individuals are confronted every day with choices, and that they have the free will to choose between alternatives;
- fifth, that freely thinking (rationally and irrationally) and freely acting (morally and immorally) individuals are capable of making decisions and acting upon them;
- sixth, at purposive human agents cause events to happen; and

- finally, that human thought and action can have intended and unintended consequences. This view of human nature suggests that individuals are morally responsible for their decisions and actions and the consequences that follow therefrom. Thus the new moral history puts the thinking back into ideas, the judgment back into intentions, and the volition back into actions."

The basic irreconcilable moral conflict between Democrat Marxists and natural rights conservatives is the very first principle of morality that Thompson cites:

Marxists do not believe that individuals are capable of making decisions about society, and seek to impose their own moral views on what they think is best for society.

Those decisions about social welfare cannot be imposed without the oppressive police power of the state to compel obedience to the Marxist vision.

Thompson describes the American Spirit of Liberty as the guiding philosophy of American patriots who fought the British for independence.

Thompson writes,

"The American "spirit of liberty" meant discovering and resisting the forces of despotism before such forces could sink roots in the New World. It was common for colonial Americans to view [tyrannical] power as restless and sleepless, which meant they must be ever alert to its machinations. The colonists frequently invoked Machiavelli's famous dictum, "Obsta princiipis" (i.e., to resist the first beginnings)."

Thompson describes the Spirit of Liberty as a philosophical mindset that is characterized by a love of individual freedom and a hatred of slavery. That mindset is the unifying first principle of the American society.

Thompson writes,

"The word "spirit" as used in the phrase signifies an action in defense of a principle, and was defined by American patriots as a sentiment, a   mindset, a disposition, and a virtue. As a sentiment, it loves freedom and hates slavery; as a mindset, it is watchful, suspicious, and skeptical; as a disposition, it is restless, protective, and vigilant; and as a virtue, it is defined by integrity, fortitude, courage, and patriotism. Taken together, the "spirit of liberty" is a sense of life defined by independence in the fullest sense of the term."

If natural rights conservatives, MAGA Trump voters and Republicans, actually had an ideology to combat Marxist collectivism, in the Marxist war on conservatives it would be this original moral value of the spirit of liberty.

But, the Democrat Marxist objective of permanent power is not going away. After Obama's transformation of the

Democrat Party, in 2012, Marxism became a permanent feature of American politics.

There is no political force that would compel Marxist Democrats to give up their quest for power, or relinquish their current hold on power, and to suddenly revert to the earlier status quo of social class economic competition, under Madison's constitution.

Madison's constitution is defective in its system of checks and balances to solve the new ideological conflict in America.

His second method of amendment requires that 34 state legislatures call for a constitutional convention. The proposed amendments must subsequently be approved by 38 state legislatures.

The obvious flaw in Madison's amendment process is as evident today, as it was when it was adopted.

Madison's fundamental flaw is that his amendment process offers no solution for citizens to directly restore the rule of law, when the central government becomes tyrannical, yet is unwilling to amend the constitution because it would disrupt the elites arbitrary power.

George Mason stated that it,

"would be improper to require the consent of the National Legislature, because they may abuse their power, and refuse their consent on that very account."

Madison agreed with Mason and promised that,

"no amendments of the proper kind would ever be obtained by the people, if the Government should become oppressive."

In The Federalist #85, Alexander Hamilton stated that when states submitted the proper number of applications, Congress was "obliged" to call a convention and that "nothing is left to the discretion of Congress."

But, the central government has become oppressive and tyrannical, and Madison's amendment process for ratification is too convoluted for citizens to overcome the oppression.

The only solution to end the Marxist tyranny in the swamp is for citizens to start over, with the socialists forming their own new nation, and natural rights conservatives restoring the original natural rights republic, based upon the principles in the Declaration of Independence

This fact constitutes the logic of an absolute divorce and permanent civil dissolution between citizens in liberty free states and citizens in Marxist socialist states.

One side of the ideological war is well-organized and already engaged in a civil war to eliminate their enemies.

The other side is stuck in the historical mirage that Madison's constitution can offer a peaceful solution to the war.

There is no longer a basis of shared moral values or allegiance to the rule of law, for holding the nation together.

The only peaceful non-violent solution is civil dissolution.

Chapter 2. The End of the American Rule of Law.

The rule of law is an unwritten allegiance that citizens will voluntarily obey a code of social behavior, based upon shared cultural values.

Each culture can have its own unique set of shared cultural values.

Or, as Fredrich Hayek would say about the American rule of law, in 1943, in The Road to Serfdom, freedom under the rule of law is:

"a condition of liberty in which all are allowed to use their knowledge for their purposes, restrained only by rules of just conduct of universal application, is likely to produce for them the best conditions for achieving their aim."

The minimal conditions for citizen allegiance to the rule of law, as developed by the legal scholar, A.V. Dicey, were:

- fidelity to constitutional rules;
- principled predictability of the behavior of government officials;
- actions embodied in valid constitutional authority.

These minimal conditions for allegiance to the rule of law follow the constitutional theory of James M. Buchanan that citizens will follow fair constitutional rules that they give to themselves.

Holding the rule of law moral values in common allows all citizens in a specific society to embrace a type of trust that all citizens, rich and poor, will follow the unwritten rules of their society.

The rule of law ended under Obama, and no constitutional force exists to compel Democrat Marxists to suddenly begin to obey the rule of law.

Even if some magical force existed to compel Democrat Marxists to resume allegiance to the original American rule of law, the weakness of Madison's constitutional framework in defending liberty would still be in effect.

It was Madison's flawed constitutional arrangement that viewed society as a economic competition between the natural aristocracy and common citizens that allowed the Democrat Marxist to seize power.

The centralized political power granted to the natural aristocracy in Madison's rules were seized by the Democrats, in the election of 2020, and they will never relinquish, peacefully, their illegitimate authority.

In Declaring Rights: A Brief History with Documents, Jake Rakove explained that in American society,

"Our rights do not depend on the constitutional text alone...citizens and officials must be imbued with the principles and norms that the constitution expresses."

What Rakove means with his term "imbued" is a widely-held cultural allegiance and loyalty that citizens and leaders will follow the cultural rules, even when that behavior may be contrary to the personal interests of an individual.

When the cultural beliefs about allegiance to the rule of law are not pervasive, and widely-held, however, the rule of law will be weak or non-existent, leading to tyranny, and rule evasion in political and legal exchanges.

Shared cultural values, in other words, provide an essential set of conditions for pro-social rule adherence in political and financial exchanges involving trust among citizens and leaders.

Yet, common cultural values that emphasize the discharge of future obligations are not sufficient, by themselves, to insure that the allegiance to the rule of law will compel obedience by citizens and government agents.

This uncertainty about obedience to the rule of law is especially relevant for cultures that have internal competing cultural values (multi-cultural).

The argument made in this chapter is that the Marxist Democrats do not hold the cultural values of individual freedom, as expressed in the Declaration, in common with natural rights conservatives.

In other words, natural rights conservatives, who believe in the shared principles of liberty, cannot trust the socialists to follow the American rule of law.

The socialists simply use the rubric of the cultural values of freedom, and lie as Obama did, as a platform to undermine and subvert the rule of law, in order to overthrow the national sovereignty of the United States.

Our argument about why the Marxist Democrats will never follow the rule of law of natural rights begins in history, in the late 1640's, with Thomas Hobbes, in The Leviathan.

Hobbes was trying to answer the question of what force would replace either the king, or the Catholic church, in performing the social function of holding dissociated individuals together in a cooperative society, and what force would compel citizen obligation to serve the public purpose.

As a method of helping him to answer his question, Hobbes created an imaginary setting called "the state of nature," and then tried to imagine what individuals in the state of nature would do for rules of social cooperation when they left the state of nature to form a civil society.

For Hobbes, what replaced the king or the church for enforcing social authority was the rule of law.

Obedience to the rules created by individuals when they left the state of nature would be enforced by a type of market-based authority called "Leviathan."

Leviathan would enforce both economic exchanges and political exchanges, pursuant to the rule of law adopted by individuals when they left the state of nature.

In other words, the values the citizens adopted when they left the state of nature held the citizens together in a common society, and Leviathan compelled obligation to follow the rules that the citizens created.

Fifty years after Hobbes wrote Leviathan, John Locke published his Two Treatises of Government, in 1690.

Locke's work was based in opposition to the absolutist government power envisioned by Hobbes, because that form of absolutism did not protect citizens from abuse by government agents in their property and personal privacy.

Locke applied the same imaginary method of the "state of nature," and answered the question about obedience to the rule of law with a different interpretation than Hobbes.

Locke defined individual freedom under the rule of law as follows:

"Freedom is constrained by laws in both the state of nature and political society. Freedom of nature is to be under no other restraint but the law of nature. Freedom of people under government is to be under no restraint apart from standing rules to live by that are common to everyone in the society and made by the lawmaking power established in it. Persons have a right or liberty to follow their own will in all things that the law has not prohibited and not be subject to the inconstant, uncertain, unknown, and arbitrary wills of others."

The goal for Locke was voluntary obedience to the rule of law that embodied moral conditions, or standards of moral conduct.

For Locke, the two basic moral conditions were protection of property from the all-powerful state, and protection of the individual liberty in the exercise of natural rights.

All "rational" citizens would want to accumulate property, thought Locke, and the most rational of citizens would want to accumulate unlimited property.

On the other hand, only irrational citizens did not want to accumulate property. And, reasoned Locke, irrational citizens would not be allowed to participate in social decisions about making or enforcing the law.

The constitutional public purpose of maintaining social order in the natural rights individualist authority pattern in

Locke is tempered by the equally important public purpose of defining social rules of cooperation allowing for each individual to define and pursue self-interest.

A rational individual, with a rational self-interest, would choose fair rules for all, aimed at the greatest freedom for all.

In constitutional decision-making under uncertainty, individuals would seek rules that had maximum equal rights for all, with special privileges for none. The end goal, or telos, of the constitution, in this case of rational self-interest, is individual freedom to pursue their life's goals.

In contrast to the goal of individual freedom, Madison sought to balance the social class conflict with rules that elevated the financial interests, and political power of the elites, over the economic interests of common citizens.

Madison falsely assumed that the natural aristocracy would not abuse their positions of authority because the ruling class possessed civic virtue.

In Madison's reasoning, the moral quality of civic virtue would allow the ruling class to place the constitutionally-undefined public purpose above their own selfish social class interests in making and enforcing social rules.

J. L. Mackie, in his book, Ethics: Inventing Right and Wrong, suggests that the ambient cultural values of social class conflict embedded in Madison's constitutional rules influences ethical decisions about following the rule of law made every day by individuals.

Individuals are continually engaged, throughout their lives, in trying to answer the question: "What sort of person is it in my interest to be?"

According to Mackie, the answer, for each individual, is influenced by the ambient culture because the culture provides the context of the social good, or the public purpose.

Madison's flawed constitutional rules failed to define, in the Preamble, the constitutional public purpose.

Creating a "more perfect union," that was better than the Articles of Confederation, could mean implementing unfair rules to benefit the ruling class, who had the power to define the public purpose.

In describing the evolution of the American version of the rule of law, Robert Hoffert, in A Politics of Tensions: The Articles of Confederation and American Political Ideas, explained that the Articles were based upon voluntary obedience to the rule of law through persuasive consent and not the coercive authority of the police power of the state [Leviathan.].

In other words, the conception of the American rule of law in the Articles of Confederation are different from the conception of the rule of law under Madison's rules.

The three most important cultural values that supported the rule of law, expressed in the Articles, according to Hoffert were:

- decentralization of legal and political power away from the central government,
- non-coercion by government agencies and elected representatives from encroaching on natural rights, and,
- the greatest priority of local government authority, in both rule and law-making, and law enforcement.

Melancton Smith, a natural rights delegate to the 1787 convention, wrote that,

"The [Madison] Constitution is radically defective. It vests in Congress "great and uncountroulable powers" that it will use "to annihilate all the state governments, and reduce this country to one single government."

Smith warned that instead of creating a balance of power, Madison's constitution would combine legislative power with judicial power that would eventually destroy the local governments.

He stated that the Supreme Court would interpret the Constitution according to the justices', "spirit and reason, and would they mold the government into any shape they please."

Hoffert cites Thomas Paine as the guiding intellectual authority for expressing the original American ideas about the rule of law.

For Paine, the natural rights republic must be built on the truth, the shared moral truth about individual liberty, not on coercive power of the government to compel obedience.

And, not on the whimsical vicarious interpretation of the public purpose, as defined by the ruling class, as they went along in time, making up rules to benefit their social class interests.

For both Paine and Jefferson, truth was reached through the convictions of open inquiry and examination.

Paine said that,

"universal moral truth must be knowable."

In other words, as Jefferson would write, the truth of equal individual liberty was logically "self-evident."

Self-evident, used in this context, is the logical conclusion, knowable by deductive reasoning, that citizens would reach about the end goals of equal liberty of their society.

For Paine, when citizens left the state of nature to form civil society and civil rights, those rights were based upon a moral rational truth of equal natural rights.

The moral rational truth, for Paine, was "knowable." For Jefferson, the truth was "self-evident."

Paine wrote,

"...for where the rights of men are equal, every man must finally see the necessity of protecting the rights of others as the most effectual security of his own rights."

It is the concept of equal individual liberty that has a shared common meaning in the American founding of 1776, which leads citizens to the logical conclusion that,

"...freedom and rights mean a perfect equality of them."

As Paine wrote, in Common Sense, the rule of law replaced the rule of the king and the Pope.

"...the world may know, that so far as we approve of monarchy, that in America THE LAW IS KING. For as in absolute governments the King is law, so in free countries the law ought to be king; and there ought to be no other. But lest any ill use should afterwards arise, let the crown at the conclusion of the ceremony be demolished, and scattered among the people whose right it is."

Voluntary obedience to the rule of law, and civil law, in the original American conception, is a means to the attainment of citizens becoming the citizen they envision themselves to be.

As Paine noted,

"Thus, law can only be means for individuals to use to accomplish their individual goals, not a means for society or the state to accomplish their goals, because these entities can have no ends of their own."

The force in a natural rights republic that compels voluntary obedience to the rule of law is individual self-interest.

Under the Articles of Confederation, American citizens would obey the rule of law because obedience serves their rational self-interest.

Madison's rules of civil procedure in his constitution create a weak version of the rule of law that was eventually usurped by the Democrat Marxists.

The centralized power of the natural aristocracy, under Madison's rules, were gained, illegitimately by the Democrat Marxists, rendering Madison's system of checks and balances ineffective against government tyranny.

Madison's "weak liberty" rule of law consists of four components:

- The rule of law means a formal, regular process of law enforcement and adjudication.
- The rule of law means general rules of law that binds obedience of all people and are promulgated and enforced by a system of courts and law enforcement, not by mere discretionary authority.
- The rule of law means "due process of law" that provides regular procedural protections and safeguards against abuse by government authority.

    No "ex post facto" laws—that is, laws that classify an act as a crime leading to punishment after the act occurs.

    No "bills of attainder," which are laws that punish individuals or groups without a judicial trial.

    Provision of "habeas corpus" No person may be imprisoned without legal cause.

    No "double jeopardy" No person can be tried or punished twice for the same crime.

- The rule of law means equality before the law. No common citizen is above the law, or beyond the reach of the law, in their obligation to follow the law.

We argue that it is this set of 4 conditions for Madison's version of the rule of law that the Marxist Democrats ended after Trump's election of November 2016.

Eli Lake, of Bloomberg News, reported that, immediately after the 2016 election,

"Susan Rice requested the identities of U.S. persons in raw intelligence reports on dozens of occasions that were connected to the Donald Trump transition and campaign, according to U.S. officials familiar with the matter."

Rice's action were the starting point of Democrats implementing the police state espionage of political opponents.

It is a criminal act for any government agent to disclose or to use information obtained in counter-espionage, if the official knew or had reason to know, that the information was obtained in an illegal manner.

From the moment Trump won, in 2016, Obama was engaged in using criminal espionage to "unmask" Trump and his aides, in order to concoct the story that Trump had engaged in treasonous behavior with the Russians.

If Obama could have made the allegation of treason stick, before Trump's inauguration, he would have been able to appoint a special prosecutor, while Obama was still President.

Obama and Rice did not have enough time, from November, 2016, to the date of the inauguration, in January, 2017, to implement his plan to appoint a special prosecutor, who would have prevented the transfer of power.

Allegiance and obedience to the rule of law in America would have required that Obama, Hillary, and Rice be prosecuted for committing multiple federal felonies.

But, the rule of law ended, resulting in a two-tiered justice system where Marxist Democrats evade criminal prosecution.

The motive and intent of Rice in unmasking the Trump administration was to leak the fake evidence of Trump's collusion with Russians, in order to provide false evidence of treason.

Obama approved Rice's criminal act of political espionage on his political enemies.

Eli Lake reports that Rice explained her unmasking project, in an interview with NBC's Andrea Mitchell.

Rice stated,

"Let me give you a hypothetical example. Let's say there was a conversation between two foreigners, about a conversation they were having with an American, who was proposing to sell them high-tech bomb making equipment."

Rice's description would have been a better fit for Hillary's behavior in selling uranium mines to the Russians, during her tenure at the U. S. State Department.

The Russian collusion fantasy that Rice concocted as justification for spying on her enemies, however, is entirely consistent with her allegiance to promoting the ideology of global socialism.

Donald Trump's MAGA doctrine is a threat to the agenda of the New World Order, and Jack Smith is the DOJ's hired gun for eliminating the Trump threat.

Jack Smith's persecution of Trump needs to be placed within this larger global context of protecting the financial interests of both the legal and illegal activities of global elites who manage the New World Order agenda.

Smith is not simply using Biden's two-tiered judicial system to eliminate a political opponent in the U. S. political system.

After the rule of law ended in America, the two-tiered justice system allows the agents of government to abuse their power for personal financial benefit.

Smith, and Biden, use their illicit power to protect their financial interests in both the legal crony corporate rent extraction in America's shared plunder political model, and also to protect the $32 billion per year organized criminal activities of the child sex slavery trade.

Both the corrupt legal rent extraction from corporate lobbying and the criminal rent extraction are so deeply embedded into the American political and judicial system that trying to modify or amend the system to return to the original concept of the American rule of law is impossible.

In his article, "A Specific Type of Continuity," Sundance explains the continuity between the protection of both the legal and illegal corruption of the U. S. government, as enforced by the deep state spy institutions. (The Last Refuge, July 21, 2023.).

The continuity that he describes is the permanent continuity of the use of the FBI/CIA police power to maintain both systems of corruption.

He writes that after the terrorist attacks of 9/11, the entire police state and judicial institutional structure of the United States was altered.

"…literally a structural reform of the entire domestic terrorist apparatus that created the Director of National Intelligence (DNI), the Department of Homeland Security (DHS) and the Transportation Safety Administration (TSA), a bill only debated for a few weeks, the baseline was the enhanced 'continuity of government' in the event of an emergency...the outcome of the Patriot Act was to create a system where every American was now viewed by our federal government through the prism of the [U. S.] citizen being a potential terrorist threat. [MAGA patriots] The federal government aligned all of our institutions and systems accordingly."

Sundance explains why the deep state New World Order has concluded that Trump and MAGA Patriots must be eliminated.

" it was the viewpoint of a very specific type of government "continuity" that led to the opposition against Donald Trump by Democrats and Republicans. Trump would be a disruptive influence if introduced into a continuation mission that did not like change. [to global corruption.]. This 'continuity' mindset then established the justification for every institution and element of the bureaucracy, including almost all layers of the people who run them, to oppose Donald Trump."

The ruling class American deep state protects the continuity of both legal and illegal corruption, and Trump threatens the continuity of the flow of wealth to New World Order elites.

From the end of the American rule of law perspective of the FBI, both forms of corruption are equally worthy of protection because both forms of corruption serve the interests of the ruling class, who determine the "public purpose" of government.

The reason that Joe Biden's criminal bribe schemes will never be investigated, or prosecuted, is that the FBI/CIA deep state is protecting Biden's criminal activity from prosecution because there is no longer allegiance to the concept of the rule of law.

The reason that we argue that a civil dissolution is the best solution for MAGA conservatives to the revolting New World Order is that there is no countervailing force in Madison's existing constitution that opposes the Marxist Democrat criminal protection racket.

As Sundance points out, rather than a countervailing force to oppose corruption, there is a unified continuity of the entire government apparatus in DOJ to protect the corruption.

As a consequence, after the Marxist Democrats seized power in 2020, the rule of law no longer exists in America.

And, there is nothing in Madison's rules which would allow the rule of law to be re-established, even if a magical force would compel Marxist Democrats to obey the constitutional rule of law, after it was re-established.

The CIA is a self-funded agency that benefits financially from the illegal criminal corruption, and the FBI protects the legal corruption of crony capitalism because their agency receives a cut from the rent extraction gained by elected representatives.

Madison's constitution is defective, beyond repair, because it does not contain the definition of liberty as the public purpose in his Preamble.

The absence of the mission of liberty in Madison's Preamble has allowed the United States government to degenerate into a disgusting reprehensible unelected tyranny, led by a pedophile who masquerades as an elected leader, who claims that he cannot resist his attraction to children.

The best solution to the end of the American rule of law is a civil dissolution, and starting over with a new constitution, at the point of history of 1776.

Chapter 3. Starting America Over At 1776.

Part of our argument about the necessity of a civil dissolution and starting over with a new constitution is that reverting to allegiance to Madison's constitution does not eradicate the permanent problem of Marxism in American politics.

It was the defects in Madison's rules that allowed the Marxists to capture the centralized, consolidated levers of government power that were originally intended to elevate the commercial and financial interests of the natural aristocracy over the interests of common citizens.

Madison's model of government was the British mixed monarchy, but without the King or multi-party parliamentary framework.

Re-imposing that British model of government, today, would not solve the problems posed by the Democrat Marxist's quest for permanent power.

Madison's American version of the unwritten British Constitution was influenced by the legal philosophy of Sir William Blackstone, who wrote Commentaries on the Laws of England.

Because the United Kingdom was a monarchy, Blackstone spent a great deal of his book explaining how the king acted as a counter-balance to the House of Lords, in the British Parliament.

Blackstone wrote,

"The king is himself a part of the parliament: and, as this is the reason of his being so, very properly therefore the share of legislation, which the constitution has placed in the crown, consists in the power of rejecting, rather than resolving."

The term used to describe the king's role in checking the power of Parliament was "Crown-in-Parliament."

The rejection of legislation by the king appeared to Madison to be a form of veto.

Blackstone wrote,

"Crown in Parliament was sovereign in all matters of concern to the British empire."

After 1687, part of the king's constitutional authority was assumed in the parliament's implementation of the prerogatives of the crown. The king's responsibility was to act as the ultimate supreme authority in British law to overrule unconstitutional acts of the Parliament.

The king's agent in Parliament was the Prime Minister, who the king appointed.

Under the unwritten British constitution, the power of Parliament was not balanced within the institutions and agencies of government.

It was balanced by the Crown in Parliament, operating outside the agencies of government, to compel obedience to the rule of law.

Blackstone wrote,

"If the Parliament of Great Britain will positively enact a thing to be done, which is unreasonable, I know of no power in the ordinary forms of the British Constitution that is vested with authority to control it."

In other words, there is no force inside the framework of the British Parliament that acts to control the actions of the Parliament.

The final, supreme arbiter of power in Great Britain is the king.

If Madison had followed Blackstone's British constitutional contract law, Madison's central government would have been an agent of 13 state government principals.

Madison eliminated the basis of the British principal-agency relationship and substituted his own version of the balance of power, where both the President and the Supreme Court had veto power over legislation.

As was the case in creating the Office of President, the fit between the model of the British constitution and Madison's constitution was not perfect.

Madison inverted the balance of power by making one of the branches of government, the Supreme Court, the ultimate judge of its own powers, and also of the powers of the Congress, the President, and the states.

In other words, the U. S. Supreme Court became the king, in Madison's model of government.

To summarize, in the case of the Office of President, Madison relied on his own version of the British prime minister for his concept of the American president.

In his concept of balanced power, Madison substituted the Supreme Court as the sole arbiter of government power, as if the Supreme Court was the Crown-in-Parlament.

When the King surrendered to the states, in Paris in 1783, he wrote,

"His Brittanic Majesty acknowledges the said United States to be free, sovereign and independent States."

The King surrendered to 13 independent states, not to "We, the people."

Madison did not accept the surrender of the King as establishing the sovereignty of states.

The terms used by the King would have forced Madison to admit that the 13 states had individual contracts with the King.

If Madison had accepted the independent sovereignty of the states, he could not have used his ruse of "We, the people."

In his attempt to evade the sovereignty of states, Madison had to ignore the founding documents of the new nation, and implement his balance of power without relying on Locke's compact theory of government.

In the first instance, Madison's new formula sought to balance the institutional powers of the three branches of government, without mentioning the Declaration of Independence.

Second, he sought to balance power between the new central government and the states, without mentioning the Articles of Confederation.

Third, he sought to use constitutional rules to balance the financial interests of the natural aristocracy and the common class, without mentioning that the natural aristocracy in America was just like the nobility of Great Britain.

All three forces were interrelated and each political force affected the other forces in Madison's scheme.

At the time of Madison's writing, in 1787, the natural rights conservatives opposed the constitution because it unfairly tilted the financial rules in favor of the natural aristocracy.

We argue that the decentralized state sovereignty framework of the Articles of Confederation would have been, then, and would be, now, a better model to protect liberty for the new government.

In An Economic Interpretation of the Constitution of the United States, Charles Beard explained that, for Madison,

"The primary objective of government [in Madison] is the making of rules which determine the property relations of members of society, the dominant classes whose rights are thus to be determined perforce obtain from government."

"Congress, in February 1787," noted Beard,

"invited the states to send delegates to a convention in Philadelphia for the "sole and express purpose of revising the Articles of Confederation."

Instead of re-writing the Articles of Confederation, Madison used the opportunity of the convention to jettison the Articles and impose his ideas of the British social class system as the constitutional arrangement for the 13 states.

In that system, the elites (natural aristocracy) had the power to make the laws, and the citizens (hurly-burly) had the duty to obey the laws made by the elites.

James Wilson, a Federalist, said during the Philadelphia Convention, in 1787 that,

"Laws may be unjust, may be unwise, may be dangerous, may be destructive; and yet not be so unconstitutional as to justify the Judges in refusing to give them effect. But with regard to every law, however unjust, oppressive or pernicious, which did not come plainly under this description, they would be under the necessity as judges to give it a free course."

Alexander Hamilton noted, in The Federalist # 78, that the federal courts,

"were designed to be an intermediate body between the people and their legislature" in order to ensure that the people's representatives acted only within the authority given to Congress under the Constitution."

In other words, as the anti-federalist Centinel asked about Madison's arrangement,

"If the people are sovereign how does the opinion of citizens direct the policies of government?"

The rules for making the laws, under Madison's framework, were safely insulated from citizen consent, yet, after the laws had been passed, no matter how unjust, citizens were compelled to obey the laws.

There is nothing in Madison's Federalist constitution, noted Centinel, like the detailed definition of consent of the citizens in the various state constitutions.

As noted by Brutus, a natural rights proponent, during the ratification debates,

"The framers of this constitution appear to have followed that of the British, in rendering the judges independent, by granting them their offices during good behaviour, without following the constitution of England, in instituting a tribunal in which their errors may be corrected; [by the King] and without adverting to this, that the judicial under this system have a power which is above the legislative, and which indeed transcends any power before given to a judicial by any free government under heaven."

Brutus reiterated this sentiment. He wrote,

"The costs of [legal representation] in the supreme court will be so great, as to put it out of the reach of the poor and middling class of citizens to contest a suit in it."

In his book, The Articles of Confederation, Merrill Jensen answers Centinel's question.

"The Federalists adopted a theory of the sovereignty of the people in the name of the people, but erected a nationalistic government whose purpose was to thwart the will of the people in whose name they act."

Few, if any of Madison's cohorts worried about the basic logical contradiction unleashed his constitutional scheme.

As Elisha Douglass noted,

"Hence, a double paradox: to preserve their own liberty, the unprivileged masses must be prevented from infringing on the privileged few; to maintain a government based on consent, a large proportion of the people must be deprived of the ability to extend or withhold consent."

As Sean Wilentz wrote in, The Rise of American Democracy: Jefferson to Lincoln,

"The people had no formal voice of their own in government. And, that was exactly how it was supposed to be – for once the electors had chosen their representatives, they ceded power, reserving none for themselves until the next election...The people, as a political entity, existed only on election day."

As Thomas Paine stated at the time, that Madison's more perfect union was, "a nominal nothing without principles."

What Paine meant was that Madison created constitutional rules of civil procedure for making political decisions, without defining the end goal, or public purpose of the constitution.

For Madison, a more perfect union consisted of imposing the British mixed monarchy, not the state sovereignty model of the Articles of Confederation.

Philanthropos, a natural rights patriot, argued that there was nothing seriously wrong with the Articles of Confederation that Madison could not have easily fixed at the convention in Philadelphia.

He stated,

"Our present constitution, [the Articles], with a few additional powers to Congress, seems better calculated to preserve the rights and defend the liberties of our citizens, than the one proposed, (by Madison), without proper amendments. Let us therefore, for once, show our judgment and solidarity by continuing it, (the Articles)."

The Articles of Confederation were adopted by the Continental Congress on November 15, 1777, and were ratified by the 13 states on March 1, 1781.

The Articles created a "perpetual union" of the 13 states. The opening paragraph, titled, A Pledge of Perpetual Union stated that "Each state must accept and agree to follow the decisions of the United States in Congress assembled. The states must follow all of the rules as stated in the Articles of Confederation. The union of states is meant to last forever."

Article XIII required all amendments to be first proposed by Congress and then ratified by all thirteen state legislatures.

Madison ignored the provisions of amendments, and evaded the rules for ratification.

Article XIII of the Articles of Confederation specified that any amendments had to be ratified by all thirteen states, in contrast to Madison's ratification process of special interest controlled conventions, in just nine states.

The Articles stated,

"And the Articles of this confederation shall be inviolably observed by every State, and the union shall be perpetual; nor shall any alteration at any time hereafter be made in any of them; unless such alteration be agreed to in a congress of the united States, and be afterwards confirmed by the legislatures of every State."

When Thomas Burke, of North Carolina, drafted his version of the new Articles of Confederation, in 1776, he presumed that the two parties to the contract were the legislatures of the states, and the as-yet created new national government.

The Articles of Confederation that he drafted provided the institutional mechanisms of representation so that the elected representatives in the national government could interpret the consent and translate the message of consent, given by the states, into central government action.

Burke proposed that all sovereign power was in the states separately and that the federal government held enumerated powers.

He wrote that each state,

"retains its sovereignty, freedom and independence...and any right which is not by this confederation expressly delegated to the United States in Congress assembled."

Burke had read as many of the new state constitutions as existed at the time, and assumed that the states would translate consent into protection of the citizen's natural rights.

For example, the Massachusetts Constitution of 1780, grants irrevocable sovereign authority to citizens in several critical areas:

- 'Section 10 of the Declaration of Rights provides that "no part of the property of any individual . . . [can] be taken from him . . . without his own consent, or that of the representative body of the people."

- 'Section 23 provides no tax can be levied "without the consent of the people, or their representatives in the legislature."
- 'Under Executive Power, the constitution prohibited the governor from sending any member of the state military out of the state, "without their free and voluntary consent, or the consent of the legislature."

George Mason believed that the new government would be legitimate only if it rested on popular sovereignty of the individual citizens, instead of Madison's deliberate privileged position of the natural aristocracy.

It was towards the end of the convention in August of 1787, that Mason realized that what Madison had in mind was to make the proposed U. S. Senate function like the British House of Lords, and to make the office of the U. S. President function like the British king, but without the King's Privy Council.

The first time Mason was able to see all of the changes made by Madison was on the morning of September 17, 1787, the last day of the Convention.

William G. Hyland, Jr. writes that at the end of the Convention,

"Mason was convinced that the fundamental principles of the Revolution stood in jeopardy." (Hyland, William G., George Mason: The Founding Father Who Gave Us The Bill of Rights, Regnery History, 2019.).

Hyland notes that towards the end of the Convention, Mason realized that,

"What is being proposed…was the creation of a central government that looks suspiciously to them just like the British government that they had been fighting against…the political system that Mason favored would ensure that the exercise of arbitrary, excessive and dictatorial power would be prevented…what Mason feared most in a central government was too powerful an executive… the president could use his patronage to corrupt Congress…the government will degenerate into a monarchy."

Mason contrasted the authentic British mixed social class conflict model of government with Madison's modified British system designed to establish an American aristocracy.

Mason argued that in the British model, the House of Lords could not dominate the King, unlike in Madison, where the President [surrogate king] and Senate were from the same social class natural aristocracy.

Mason reasoned that, if Madison was intent on replicating the British model of government, then the President should have a Council of State to check the power of a rogue President.

Brent Tarter writes,

"In the opinion of Mason, imperfections in the structure of the British government had undermined the once sound principles of the [unwritten] British constitution and allowed corruption to disrupt or destroy the well-balanced system that mixed the three estates of society [royalty, nobility and commons] in a government of interlocking executive, legislative and judicial institutions." (Tarter, Brent, George Mason and the Conservation of Liberty, The Virginia Magazine of History and Biography, July 1991.).

Mason had written, in the Fairfax Resolves, that,

"The most important and valuable part of the British Constitution, upon which its very existence depends, is, the fundamental principle of the people being governed by no laws to which they have not given their consent by Representatives freely chosen by themselves, who are affected by the laws they enact equally with their constituents, to whom they are accountable, and whose burthens they [the elected representatives] share, in which consists the safety and happiness of the community; for if this part of the [British] Constitution was taken away or materially altered the government must degenerate either into an absolute and despotic monarchy, or a tyrannical aristocracy, and the freedom of the people be annihilated."

The delayed realization by Mason about Madison's plan during the convention was primarily because a small committee of detail had not shared the final version of the draft document about the function of the President with the other delegates.

By the time Mason and the other delegates finally saw the Brearly Committee's last unfinished draft, on September 4, 1787, there was no time left in the convention for Mason to change the draft in the open debate, because the other delegates would not second, or refused to vote, on Mason's motions to open debate.

However, even after September 4, the final document continued to be changed and modified, in secret, up until the night of September 16, 1787, when Madison inserted the revised Fugitive Slave clause, which had been deleted in the previous open debates, in late August.

During the Convention, in the debates about the power of the President, in late August, Mason argued,

"It seems as if it were taken for granted that all offices will be filled by the Executive, while I think many will remain in the gift of the legislature. In either case it is necessary to shut the door against corruption. If otherwise, they [the Senate] may make or multiply places in order to fill them. . . . We must, in the present system remove the temptation [of corruption]. I admire many parts of the British constitution and government, but I detest their corruption. Why has the power of the crown increased, so remarkably increased, the last century?"

Gordon Wood observed that,

"Mason feared corruption at any level of government more than he feared the consolidation of power in a national government....The thirst of power will prevail to oppress the people. Bribery and corruption will be practiced in America more than in England." (Wood, Gordon, The Making of the Constitution, Baylor University Press, 1987.).

David Siemers noted that, on September 15, 1787, the last day of open debate at the Convention, Mason stated,

"The plan of amendments is exceptionable and dangerous. As the proposing of amendments in both modes to depend in the first immediately and in the second ultimately on Congress, no amendments of the proper kind would ever be obtained by the people, if the Government should become oppressive, as he verily believed would be the case." (Siemers, David J., The Antifederalists: Men of Great Faith and Forbearance, 2003.).

At the very end of the Convention, Mason repeatedly warned the other delegates that Madison's rules would lead to a corrupt centralized aristocratic elite tyranny.

From Madison's notes:

Mr. RANDOLPH. We have in some revolutions of this plan made a bold stroke for Monarchy. We are now doing the same for an aristocracy. He dwelt on the tendency of such an influence in the Senate over the election of the President in addition to its other powers, to convert that body into a real & dangerous Aristocracy.

Col: MASON. As the mode of appointment is now regulated, he could not forbear expressing his opinion that it is utterly inadmissible. He would prefer the Government of Prussia to one which will put all power into the hands of seven or eight men, and fix an Aristocracy worse than absolute monarchy. The words "and of their giving their votes" being inserted on motion for that purpose, after the words "The Legislature may determine the time of chusing and assembling the electors."

September 7. Col: MASON said that in rejecting a Council to the President we were about to try an experiment on which the most despotic Governments had never ventured. The Grand Signor himself had his Divan. He moved to postpone the consideration of the clause in order to take up the following:

"That it be an instruction to the Committee of the States to prepare a clause or clauses for establishing an Executive Council, as a Council of State, for the President of the U.

States, to consist of six members, two of which from the Eastern, two from the middle, and two from the Southern States, with a Rotation and duration of office similar to those of the Senate; such Council to be appointed by the Legislature or by the Senate."

September 8. A Committee was then appointed by Ballot to revise the stile of and arrange the articles which had been agreed to by the House. The committee consisted of Mr. Johnson, Mr. Hamilton, Mr. Govr. Morris, Mr.Madison and Mr. King.

September 15. [the last day of open debate] Col: MASON. 2ded. & followed Mr. Randolph in animadversions on the dangerous power and structure of the Government, concluding that it would end either in monarchy, or a tyrannical aristocracy; which, he was in doubt, but one or other, he was sure. This Constitution had been formed without the knowledge or idea of the people. A second Convention will know more of the sense of the people, and be able to provide a system more consonant to it. It was improper to say to the people, take this or nothing.

Mason's language for describing Madison's British model scheme, on September 15, "take this or nothing," went directly to the heart of Madison's duplicity in creating his constitution, without providing citizens an alternative form of government, even the most limited choice between Madison's document and the Articles of Confederation.

The entire body of delegates, prior to the appointment of the Committee on Style, on September 8, had not reached agreement or debated the powers of the Presidency, because the Brearly Committee of September 4, did not include the finished clauses about the powers of the Presidency.

The Committee on Style never released the final clauses of Article II, on the Presidency to the delegates, before they voted on them, on the final day of open debate, on September 15.

Mason stated that,

"Considering the powers of the President & those of the Senate, if a coalition should be established between these two branches, they will be able to subvert the Constitution."

As Mason's fellow natural rights compatriot, Brutus wrote,

"The judiciary under this system will have a power which is above the legislative, and which indeed transcends any power before given to a judicial by any free government under heaven."

Patrick Henry predicted that centralized tyranny would be the outcome for common, middle class citizens in Madison's centralized Leviathan.

In his June 5, 1788, speech against ratification, Henry stated,

"It [Madison's constitution] is otherwise most clearly a consolidated government... the principles of this system are extremely pernicious, impolitic, and dangerous...The rights of conscience, trial by jury, liberty of the press, all your immunities and franchises, all pretensions to human rights and privileges, are rendered insecure...Did you ever read of any revolution in a nation, brought about by the punishment of those in power, inflicted by those who had no power at all? where a few neighbors cannot assemble without the risk of being shot by a hired soldiery, [IRS agents] the engines of despotism...I dread the operation of it on the middling and lower classes of people. It is for them I fear the adoption of this [Madison's] system."

At the end of his speech in the Virginia legislature, against ratification, Henry quoted the passage in Virginia's constitution, written by George Mason, which describes a natural, God-given right of citizens:

Henry stated,

"Let me read that clause of the Bill of Rights of Virginia which relates to this: third clause. "That Government is or ought to be instituted for the common benefit, protection, and security of the people, nation, or community: Of all the various modes and forms of Government, that is best which is capable of producing the greatest degree of happiness and safety, and is most effectually secured against the danger of mal-administration, and that whenever any Government shall be found inadequate, or contrary to those purposes, ***a majority of the community hath, an indubitable, unalienable, and indefeasible right to reform, alter, or abolish it, in such manner as shall be judged most conducive to the public weal.***" This, Sir, is the language of democracy; that a majority of the community have a right to alter their Government when found to be oppressive."

In The Framers Coup, Michael Klarman, (2016), noted the statement of another anti-federalist,

"The Georgia antifederalist stated that the constitution paves the way for an aristocratical government whereby about 70 nabobs would lord over 3 million citizens as slaves. In "rule by the wealthy."

Melancton Smith, another natural rights delegate to the convention, wrote that,

"The Constitution is radically defective. It vests in Congress great and uncountroulable powers that it will use to annihilate all the state governments, and reduce this country to one single government."

Smith warned that instead of creating a balance of power, Madison's constitution would combine ruling class legislative power with judicial power that would eventually destroy the local and state governments.

He stated that the Supreme Court would interpret the Constitution according to the justices', "spirit and reason, [ruling class ideology] and they would mold the government into any shape they please."

The judicial system, in other words, was designed from the get-go, to be the exclusive province of the wealthy elite, who had the money to pursue justice, and who would, subsequently, use that legal power to deprive common citizens of their property, as in the debt-lien system applied against common farmers, in the 1880s.

As Forrest McDonald explains,

"In the English system each branch of government represented people whose status was inherited…In the United States, there was no hereditary status…therefore [Madison's] the English model was inappropriate…[The British] constitution separated the people from government in two ways: some officials were chosen directly [by the aristocracy]; there was also the time barrier…there was no way for the people could express their will directly and immediately." (McDonald. Forrest, A Constitutional History of the United States. 1982.).

Philanthropos wrote, Madison's constitution would allow,

"The people are to be fleeced, and the public business neglected. From despotism and tyranny, good Lord deliver us."

Madison's rules created the legal framework for elite rule, and Hamilton then added the banking and financial system that benefitted the plutocracy as a result of money supply and interest rate manipulation.

As Goodwyn notes, in The Populist Moment,

"The ultimate monopoly was the money trust, a banking system of private plunder anchored in a metallic currency and assured of political power because it [Ruling Class] owned both sound money parties…The destruction of the cooperatives by the banks was a decisive blow, for it weakened the interior structure of [the Agrarian] democracy."

Melancton Smith, of New York, wrote in 1788, that the common citizens would not have a chance to prosper under Madison's rules.

Smith wrote,

"This will be a government of oppression. I am convinced that this government is so constituted, that the representatives will generally be composed of the first class in the community, which I shall distinguish by the name of the natural aristocracy of the country. I do not mean to give offence by using this term. I am sensible this idea is treated by many gentlemen as chimerical. I shall be asked what is meant by the natural aristocracy, and told that no such distinction of classes of men exists among us. [all in this together]. It is true it is our singular felicity, that we have no legal or hereditary distinctions of this kind; but still there are real differences: Every society naturally divides itself into classes. The author of nature has bestowed on some greater capacities than on others—birth, education, talents and wealth, create distinctions among men as visible and of as much influence as titles, stars and garters. In every society, men of this class will command a superior degree of respect—and if the government is so constituted as to admit but few to exercise the powers of it, it will, according to the natural course of things, be in their hands. Men in the middling class, who are qualified as representatives, will not be so anxious to be chosen as those of the first. When the number is so small the office will be highly elevated and distinguished—the style in which the members live will probably be high—circumstances of this kind, will render the place of a representative not a desirable one to sensible, substantial men, who have been used, to walk in the plain and frugal paths of life."

Smith continues his article by describing Madison's flawed rendition of the "extended republic."

Smith writes,

Besides, the influence of the great [ruling class] will generally enable them to succeed in elections—it will be difficult to combine a district of country containing 30 or 40,000 inhabitants, frame your election laws as you please, in any one character; unless it be in one of conspicuous military civil, or legal talents. [ruling class]. The great easily form associations; the poor and middling class form them with difficulty If the elections be by plurality, as probably will be the case in this state, it is almost certain, none but the great will be chosen—for they easily unite their interests—The common people will divide, and their divisions will be promoted by the others. There will be scarcely a chance of their uniting, in any other but some great man, unless in some popular demagogue, who will probably be destitute of principle. A substantial yeoman of sense and discernment, will hardly ever be chosen. From these remarks it appears that the government will fall into the hands of the few and the great. This will be a government of oppression."

It was the defects in Madison's rules that allowed the Marxists to capture the centralized, consolidated levers of government power that were originally intended to elevate the commercial and financial interests of the natural aristocracy over the interests of common citizens.

Given the current corruption of the uni-party deep state, it is still a government of oppression against the interests of middle and working class citizens.

The difference today is that the levers of government oppression are now in the hands of the Marxist Democrats, who seek permanent power.

Re-instituting Madison's flawed British social class conflict model of government, even if the Marxist Democrats agreed to abide by the rule of law, does not remedy the unfair rules on behalf of the ruling class that limit the attainment of prosperity for middle class American common citizens.

Madison's convention in 1787 was held in secret, with doors locked and window blinds shut.

The common citizens in America did not see the full set of notes and transcripts of what transpired in Madison's convention until 1911, when Max Farrand published his Records of Federal Convention of 1787.

Madison held his notes of the convention in secret until his death in 1836.

Two years after his death, his estate released a semi-public set of his notes, which Madison admitted to revising during his retirement to better reflect upon his reputation and virtue.

Two centuries of American academic historians have spun a false myth about the founding of America, citing Madison as the "Mind of the Founder."

The authentic founding occurred in 1776, not 1787.

What Madison imposed on American citizens was the British social class conflict model of government that George Mason correctly noted was contrary to the principles of liberty of the American Revolution.

A better idea for a constitution, then, would have been to improve the original constitution, based upon principles of decentralized state sovereignty, and shared cultural values of individual liberty.

A better idea for a new constitution, now, is to start over, at 1776, with a civil dissolution, and re-creating the framework of a decentralized state sovereignty consistent with principles of the Articles of Confederation, and Mason's Fairfax Resolves.

Chapter 4. Replacing Madison's Rules of Civil Procedure In Order to Enshrine Liberty As The Constitutional Public Purpose.

In order to install a centralized national government designed to benefit the natural aristocracy, Madison had to start over, with a new constitution.

This is similar in concept today to how natural rights conservatives in America need to start over, at 1776.

The rules in the Articles of Confederation had created a "perpetual union" and they were too cumbersome for Madison's revolutionary mission to elevate the financial interests of the natural aristocracy over the interests of common citizens.

The original intent of Madison's constitution is easily traced from the Annapolis Convention, in 1786, to the Philadelphia convention.

At the Annapolis convention, delegates from 5 states met, purportedly to discuss river navigation rights.

Rather than discuss river navigation, the self-selected elites in Annapolis agreed that they needed to replace the Articles with a stronger, central government, which protected the elite's financial interests, and eliminated the paper currency issued by states.

In the elite's concept of the new republic, the only function of common citizens was to vote every four years on the elites who would represent them.

Madison's subterfuge of starting over with an entirely new constitution was a well-known fact of the 51 delegates who initially met in Philadelphia.

Of the 75 delegates initially appointed by their state to attend the Convention, only 51 actually showed up.

While 95% of the citizens at the time were farmers, not one farmer was present at the convention. The delegates were drawn exclusively from the rich and well-born, intent on placing a saddle on the backs, and riding the common citizens, with spurs and whips.

By the end on the Convention, on September 17, 1787, the majority of the 75 delegates had left in disgust at what was being proposed, leaving only 38 delegates to sign the document.

When Nathan Dane, the representative from Massachusetts departed from the Convention, he stated,

"Madison's constitution appears to be intended as an entire system in itself, and not as any part of, or alteration in the Articles of Confederation" the Congress was powerless to take any action thereon."

Elbridge Gerry, from Massachusetts, speaking about Madison's Virginia resolution to establish a new centralized national government stated,

"The commission from Massachusetts empowers the deputies to proceed agreeably to the recommendation of Congress. This is the foundation of the convention. If we have a right to pass this resolution we have a right to annihilate the confederation."

Madison's motivation for "fixing" the Articles was based on the purported weakness in the Articles that allowed farmers to pay their taxes and their loan debts in paper money issued by the states.

Madison, and the 38 ruling class elites who wrote the new constitution, wanted to be paid in gold and silver, not paper money. In order to accomplish this goal, the elites had to eviscerate the legal authority of the states to issue money.

By the supreme law of the land, Madison's constitution forced the farmers to pay in gold. And, the penalty for not paying their debts in gold, was confiscation of their land by the new central government.

This technique of elites obtaining farmer's land explains the huge accumulations of land by the natural aristocracy during the period of time after 1789, and the ensuing rampant asset speculation that continues to plague the operation of the U. S. financial system.

The same legal technique of confiscation of common farmer's lands worked well after the Civil War in the debt-lien system of debt peonage, when the plantation elite consolidated their holdings of land owned by the common farmers in the South.

When farmer's failed to "pay out" at harvest time, the local merchants and bankers took the farmer's land.

In order to protect the new government from the "tyranny of the common class majority," who sought to oppress the "minority" of elites by being paid in paper money, Madison insulated the political decisions of government from common citizens.

The federalist fraud of over throwing the Articles of Confederation consisted of 3 inter-related illegal acts the federalists committed in implementing their new form of government.

1. The delegates from each state exceeded their authority granted to them by their state legislatures to "fix" the Articles. The delegates from Massachusetts were instructed by their legislature to "solely" amend the Articles of Confederation to "render the federal constitution adequate to the exigencies of government and the preservation of the union."

The Empire State's delegates were under the same instructions as those from Massachusetts. Several weeks into the Philadelphia convention, two of the New York delegates realized Madison's fraud and left, leaving only Alexander Hamilton.

Hamilton was prohibited, by the instructions of his legislature, from casting any votes, without the other two delegates being present.

Instead of following his instructions, Hamilton signed the new constitution, on behalf of New York.

Hamilton later argued that he had not exceeded his authority, knowing in advance that he was lying.

In Federalist #78, Hamilton explained the importance that he attached to acting within his delegated authority. Hamilton wrote,

"There is no position which depends on clearer principles, than that every act of a delegated authority, contrary to the tenor of the commission under which it is exercised, is void."

In other words, Hamilton argues in #78 that his signing of the finished document, on behalf of New York, according to Hamilton, was "void."

George Mason, the delegate from Virginia, stated that the delegates were "appointed for the special purpose of revising and amending the federal con-stitution, so as to obtain and preserve the important objects for which it was instituted."

When Mason discovered the intent of Madison to overthrow the Articles, he refused to sign the finished document.

2.   The 51 elites in Philadelphia adopted an illegal process to ratify the new constitution. Even though the delegates acted under the authority of the states, they never asked either Congress or the state legislatures to approve the proposed Constitution.

Rather than follow the constitutional process of amending the Articles, the federalists adopted a resolution for separate ratifying conventions to be held in each state.

Their resolutions for ratification were placed in a separate document that was not attached to the main finished document submitted to Congress.

The contents of Articles XXII and XXIII were passed, in secret deliberations, as a separate formal act adopted unanimously as an official act of the Convention.

The resolutions for ratification presented a unique, revolutionary process. The resolutions stated,

"The ratification of the Conventions of nine States shall be sufficient for the establishment of this Constitution between the States so ratifying the same."

While the rules adopted required nine states for ratification, four states did not ratify.

Congress subsequently sent those partial documents to each state, with no recommendations on how each state could proceed with calling the extra-legal ratifying conventions.

The resolutions did not contain safeguards on how the delegates in each state would be selected, resulting in special interest manipulation by the federalists to stack the conventions with supporters of Madison's arrangement.

The selection of delegates in several states was done in secret, not by the vote of the citizens.

In other words, the ratifying conventions did not derive their authority from "the consent of the governed."

The delegates to the state ratifying conventions derived their authority to ratify the new constitution from a grant of authority that they gave to themselves.

As noted by Federal Farmer,

"Pennsylvania appointed principally those men who are esteemed aristocratical…Ten other states appointed men principally connected with commerce and the judicial department. In the nature of things, nine times in ten, men of elevated classes in the community only can be chosen—Connecticut, for instance, will have five representatives—not one man in a hundred of those who form the democratic branch in the state legislature, will on a fair computation, be one of the five—The people of this country, in one sense, may all be democratic; but if we make the proper distinction between the few men of wealth and abilities, and consider them, as we ought, as the natural aristocracy of the country, and the great body of the people, the middle and lower classes, as the democracy; this federal representative branch will have but very little democracy in it, even this small representation is not secured on proper principles. . ." (Kaminsky John, and Leffler, Richard, ed., Federalists and Antifederalists: The Debate Over the Ratification of the Constitution, 1998.).

Federal Farmer's insights into the coherent social class ideology of the natural aristocracy documents their existing social class power to overthrow the government.

Federal Farmer wrote,

In my idea of our natural aristocracy in the United States, I include about four or five thousand men; and among these I reckon those who have been placed in the offices of governors, of members of Congress, and state senators generally, in the principal officers of Congress, of the army and militia, the superior judges, the most eminent professional men, &c. and men of large property*—the other. persons and orders in the community form the natural democracy; this includes in general the yeomanry, the subordinate officers, civil and military, the fishermen, mechanics and traders, many of the merchants and professional men. It is easy to perceive that men of these two classes, the aristocratical, and democratical, with views equally honest, have sentiments widely different, especially respecting public and private expences, salaries, taxes, &c. Men of the first class associate more extensively, have a high sense of honor, possess abilities, ambition, and general knowledge: men of the second class are not so much used to combining great objects; they possess less ambition, and a larger share of honesty: their dependence is principally on middling and small estates, industrious pursuits, and hard labour, while that of the former is principally on the emoluments of large estates, and of the chief offices of government. Not only the efforts of these two great parties are to be balanced, but other interests and parties also, which do not always oppress each other merely for want of power, and for fear of the consequences; though they, in fact, mutually depend on each other; yet such are their general views, that the merchants alone would never fail to make laws favourable to themselves and oppressive to the farmers, &c. the farmers alone would act on like principles; the former would tax the land, the latter, the trade. The manufacturers are often disposed to contend for monopolies, buyers make every exertion to lower prices, and sellers to raise them; men who live by fees and salaries endeavour to raise them, and the part of the people who pay them, endeavour to lower them; the public creditors to augment the taxes, and the people at large to lessen them."

Kaminsky and Leffler cite the article by Centinel about the secret political work by the natural aristocracy to overthrow the Articles of Confederation.

Centinel writes,

In many of the states, particularly in this and the northern states, there are aristocratic junto's of the well-born few, who had been zealously endeavouring since the establishment of their [state] constitutions, to humble that offensive upstart, equal liberty; but all their efforts were un-availing, the ill-bred churl [common citizens] obstinately kept his assumed station… A comparison of the authority under which the convention acted, and their form of government will show that they have despised their delegated power, [to amend the Articles of Confederation] and assumed sovereignty; that they have entirely annihilated the old confederation, and the particular governments of the several states, and instead thereof have established one general government that is to pervade the union; constituted on the most unequal principles, destitute of accountability to its constituents, and as despotic in its nature, as the Venetian aristocracy; a government that will give full scope to the magnificent designs of the well-born; a government where tyranny May glut its vengeance on the low-born, unchecked by an odious bill of rights: as has been fully illustrated in my two preceding numbers."

In Pennsylvania, when the delegates to the ratifying convention learned of the fraud for ratification, they refused to attend, causing a lack of quorum.

The federalists in Pennsylvania sent out the secret police to restrain two delegates, against their will, and held them against their will at the convention, in order to preserve the subterfuge of a legitimate quorum.

The state's rights leaders, like George Mason, called the ratification fraud of Madison's nationalists exactly what it was. Mason wrote,

"this outrageous violation employed all the arts of insinuation, and influence, to betray the people of the United States."

In the only actual vote of citizens in any state on the new constitution, the citizens of Rhode Island rejected the Constitution by a vote of 2,714 to 238.

The citizens of North Carolina's, at their 1788 convention, refused to adopt the constitution because it did not contain a citizen's Bill of Rights.

While Madison and Hamilton argued in their Federalist Papers that no state was bound to obey the Constitution until its people gave their consent, the federalists coerced and subjugated the citizens of North Carolina, over a period of three years, to force the state to submit to the illegal authority of Madison's constitution.

The federalists used their financial power on exports to manipulate and coerce North Carolina into ratifying the constitution, in 1791.

3. The revolutionary character of what Madison did to overthrow the government is evident in that Madison disconnected the text of the new constitution from the founding document, The Declaration of Independence.

The American Declaration established the clear legal supremacy of the states. The States created the Union. The States created the Articles of Confederation. The States appointed the first members of Congress.

Madison substituted a British social class system that was based upon the supremacy of the elites.

Because the British social class mixed system empowered the elites, from the get-go, that same social class of American elites were able to obtain unchecked, unelected power.

After the stolen election of 2020, that same set of unfair rules would also allow global socialists to obtain unchecked power in the deep state apparatus to impose their socialist tyranny.

Madison formed a branch of government, called the Senate, which would always be in the hands of the "virtuous" natural aristocracy."

"The delegates frequently referred to the Senate as the "aristocratic "body in the legislature, Deigned to restrain or balance the turbulent lower or "democratic" house. The Senate was meant to represent and protect "wealth," there was even the suggestion that membership therein be conditional on the ownership of considerable property. The proposal was rejected, as was a suggestion that legislators not be paid a salary, to encourage only the wealthy to submit their names as candidates." (Slonim, Shlomo, Framers' Construction/Beardian Deconstruction, Essays on the Constitutional Design of 1787, 2001.).

And, Madison created a federal judiciary that was never subject to recall or vote by the commoners. The natural aristocracy in the Senate had sole power to approve the judges, for a term of life.

Madison admits, during the debates in the Convention that the American common citizens had not yet formed themselves into a coherent social class, like the common citizens in Europe.

Madison anticipated that the common citizens would eventually form themselves into a social class with a coherent middle class ideology, and that his rules were designed to thwart that future circumstance.

"Madison said: The three principle classes. into which our citizens are divisible, were the landed, the commercial, & the manufacturing. The 3rd, class bears as yet a small proportion to the first. Their number however will daily increase. We see in the populous Countries in Europe what we shall be hereafter…in process of time, when we approximate to the kingdoms of Europe; when the number of landholders shall be comparatively small, through the various means of trade and manufactures, and not the landed interest be overbalanced in future elections, and unless provided against, what will become of your government? In England, *if elections were open to all classes of people, the property of the landed proprietors would be insecure. An agrarian law would soon take place. If these observations be just, our government ought to secure the permanent threats of the country against innovation. [common citizens].* Landholders ought to have a share of the government to support these invaluable interests and to balance and check the other. They ought to be so constituted as to protect the minority of the population against the majority. The senate, therefore, ought to be this body; In order to answer these purposes, they ought to have permanency and stability. Those have been the propositions; but my opinion is, the longer they continue in in office, the better will these views be answered." (From Farrand Records, vol. 1, pp. 421-423.Italized text added).

As Madison wrote in Federalist #48,

"It is agreed on all sides, [federalists and anti-federalists] that the powers properly belonging to one of the departments, ought not to be directly and compleatly administered by either of the other departments. It is equally evident, that neither of them ought to possess directly or indirectly, an overruling influence over the others in the administration of their respective powers."

As Madison wrote in Federalist #51,

"the great security against a gradual concentration of the several powers in the same department, consists in giving to those who administer each department, the necessary constitutional means, and personal motives, to resist encroachments of the others…"which to a certain extent is admitted on all hands to be essential to the preservation of liberty. It is evident that each department should have a will of its own…"

The "liberty" that Madison describes in #51 is not the liberty of common citizens.

The liberty Madison means is the liberty of the natural aristocracy not to have property infringed by the majority vote of common citizens in the House of Representatives.

Liberty, for common citizens, was not an enumerated right in the same way that owning slaves was an enumerated right for the natural aristocracy.

The right to own slaves was one of the provisions that could not be altered or amended under the provisions of Article V.

In other words, owning slaves was both an enumerated right of property, and a permanent, unalterable right, under Madison's rules.

We argue that the enumerated rights of property to own slaves was stronger than the unenumerated right of liberty, in Madison's constitution.

"In order to lay a due foundation for that separate and distinct exercise of the different powers of government," wrote Madison,

"The (geographical) extent of the country and number of people comprehended under the same government so that the society itself will be broken into so many parts interests and classes of citizens that the rights of the individuals or of the minority will be in little danger from interested combinations or the majority."

The vaunted and much discussed "extended republic," was not designed to bring more common citizens into the government. It was designed by Madison to prevent common citizens from ever forming a social class ideology, like the common citizens in England by breaking up those interests from forming a combination of the majority.

Madison's goal was to prevent the "tyrannical concentration of all the powers of government" in the elected hands in the House of Representatives.

In Federalist #68, Madison explained how defined executive powers would be limited in the new U.S. Constitution:

Madison writes,

"unless these departments be so far connected and blended, as to give to each a constitutional control over the others, the degree of separation...essential to a free government can never in practice be duly maintained."

Farrand notes that Charles Pinckney, a delegate from South Carolina, also assumed that the as-yet-created American common citizen ideology would eventually replicate the social class structure of England, which would threaten the existing social class ideology of the ruling class.

Pinckney is quoted, during the Convention,

"The United States is divided into three different classes: (1) professional men, (2) commercial: men, and (3) "The landed interest, the owners and cultivators are the, and ought ever to be the governing spring in the system over the commercial class.

Pinckney said:

"If that commercial policy [favoring the landed interests] is pursued, conceive it to be the true one, the merchants of this Country will not for a considerable time have much: weight in the political scale."

Slonin quotes Gouverneur Morris, an aristocrat delegate from New York, who strangely represented Pennsylvania, as almost giddy at the thought of oppressing the common citizens.

Slonin quotes Morris,

"The Rich will strive to establish their dominion and enslave the rest. They always did. They always will. The proper security agst. them is to form them into a separate interest. The two forces will then controul each other. Let the rich mix with the poor and in a Commercial Country, they will establish an Oligarchy... By thus combining &

setting, apart, the aristocratic interest, the popular interest will be combined agst. it. There will be a mutual check and mutual security [for the ruling class]. (Slonim, 2001.).

Madison feared the "people" in their collective capacity as citizens, and his representative republic sought to limit the citizen's influence in the day-to-day operations of government.

Madison stated that his representative republic was based upon

"the delegation of the government...to a small numbers of citizens, elected by the rest."

Madison wrote that his system would work well, if

"there was unequal access by those without power to adjudicate justice by making claims against those who had institutional power (natural aristocracy)."

Madison over-weighted the authority of the natural aristocracy in his constitutional arrangement so that the elite could make collective decisions for the benefit of the entire society.

As described by Robert Horwitz, in The Moral Foundations of the American Republic, Madison thought that, if the working class did not develop a class consciousness, like the common citizens of England, that they would not devolve into a dangerous "faction," one of Madison's favorite terms.

Horowitz wrote that Madison thought that,

"If all citizens (working class) have the same impulse of passion and interest (of plundering the system) they would not divide into oppressive and dangerous factions... if (working class) Americans can be made to divide themselves according to their narrow economic interests they will avoid the fatal factionalism."

As Madison noted,

"the central function of the legal system is to protect autonomous individuals (elites) from the "tyranny of the majority" (working class)."

The essence of the rule of law in Madison's arrangement is special financial group interest negotiation over the distributing the spoils of plunder.

The elites shared a common cultural value that the end goal of the British Social Class political model was to allow them to plunder the system by distributing the pie.

The flaw in Madison's Constitution is that property rights, under Madison's Constitution, could be obtained in an orderly parliamentary manner, without the benefit of shared faith or obligation to obey the rule of law that served to protect natural rights and liberty of common citizens.

Protection of property rights, in conjunction with the moral value of shared plunder, did not provide an essential set of conditions for pro-social rule adherence involving trust among citizens and leaders.

Rather, Madison's rules of separation of power were the instruments to balance and check factional political power in order to insure that social elites, the natural leaders, who made important decisions on behalf of all society, were insulated from the democratic tyranny that could be imposed by the majority of common people.

Madison's rules of civil procedure were supplemented by Hamilton's banking and monetary system, based upon elite plunder and corruption.

During his dinner with Jefferson, in 1792, to discuss the chartering of the First National Bank, Hamilton candidly told Jefferson that Madison's system of government would not work without the essential ingredient of corruption and special interest plunder provided by a banking system modeled on the Bank of England.

Hamilton, in Federalist # 65, also warned that during impeachment proceedings, it would be difficult for Congress to act solely in the interests of the nation and resist political pressure to remove a popular official, under Article II.

Hamilton correctly raised the issue, in 1788, presented by Hobbes, in 1648, of how the new government would compel obedience to the rule of law. Hamilton understood that no army, or police power alone, is sufficient to compel obedience to the constitutional rules.

Gordon Wood, in The Creation of the American Republic, cited Hamilton in Federalist # 35 on the logical justification of elite rule.

"What justified elite rule, together with the notion of virtual representation," noted Wood,

"was Hamilton's sense that all parts of the society were of a piece, that all ranks and degrees were organically connected...the state was a cohesive organic entity with a single homogeneous interest in a chain in such a way that those on the top were necessarily involved in the welfare of those below them."

In Federalist # 57, Madison and Hamilton wrote that the most important barriers to the elevation of traitors to the public liberty were frequent elections and a "limitation of the term of appointments."

However, in two of the original branches of government, the Senate and the Supreme Court, there were no term limits. The only branch of government with term limits was the House of Representatives, which was intended to keep the common citizens from forming a social class interest, like the natural aristocracy.

In other words, the shared value of plunder in Madison replaced pro-social rule allegiance to the rule of law in the Articles of Confederation.

We argue that a better idea today is to replace Madison's rules by re-constituting the principle of consent of the governed in the Articles of Confederation.

In the Declaration, Jefferson used the term "consent of the governed" to describe the legitimate form of authority in government that he proposed for the new nation. In his usage, "consent of the governed" presumes that citizens possess the rationality to provide consent in two different periods of time.

Jefferson relied on Locke to express his phrase "deriving their just powers from the consent of the governed."

In his Second Treatise of Government, Locke identified the basis of a legitimate government.

According to Locke, a ruler gains authority through the consent of the governed. The duty of that government is to protect the natural rights of the people, which Locke believed to include life, liberty, and property.

If the government should fail to protect these rights, its citizens would have the right to overthrow that government.

Both Jefferson and Locke believed in the right of citizens to abolish government.

Locke wrote:

"When the Government is dissolved, the People are at liberty to provide for themselves, by erecting a new Legislative, differing from the other, by the change of Persons, or Form, or both as they shall find it most for their safety and good. For the Society can never, by the fault of another, lose the Native and Original Right it has to preserve itself, which can only be done by a settled Legislative, and a fair and impartial execution of the Laws made by it. But the state of Mankind is not so miserable that they are not capable of using this Remedy, till it be too late to look for any. To tell People they may provide for themselves, by erecting a new Legislative, when by Oppression, Artifice, or being delivered over to a Foreign Power, their old one is gone, is only to tell them they may expect Relief, when it is too late, and the evil is past Cure. This is in effect no more than to bid them first be Slaves, and then to take care of their Liberty; and when their Chains are on, tell them, they may act like Freemen. This, if barely so, is rather Mockery than Relief; and Men can never be secure from Tyranny, if there be no means to escape it, till they are perfectly under it: And therefore it is, that they have not only a Right to get out of it, but to prevent it."

We argue that conservatives, today, have no constitutional method to escape Marxist tyranny.

The original consent, according to Locke, is given when citizens leave the state of nature to form a new government. The citizens consent among themselves to grant part of their natural, God-given rights to the new government, in order to secure a greater level of security against tyranny.

The second grant of consent occurs between citizens and the new government, from the moment the new government begins operation until the government is abolished, by the citizens.

The term "consent" also implies an on-going two-way agreement between those giving their consent, and the other party to the contract, those who agree to discharge obligations, in accordance with the initial grant of consent.

In other words, "consent of the governed" appears in the Declaration as expressing mutual obligations and duties to both parties to the contract. We defined this mutual obligation as allegiance to obey the unwritten rule of law.

The way that Jefferson used the concept implies a certain type of social reciprocity based upon the duty to reciprocate equal liberty. Jefferson emphasized this reciprocity in his writings about the civil foundations of the new nation.

Jefferson wrote,

"What is here a right towards men, is a duty towards the Creator. It is the duty of every man to render to the Creator such homage and such only as he believes to be acceptable to him. This duty is precedent, both in order of time and in degree of obligation, to the claims of Civil Society."

Rational individuals continue to obey social rules when they have mutual dependency on sharing benefits with other citizens.

Self-government, according to Jefferson, meant allowing citizens a sphere of sovereignty that could not be disrupted by the central government. Jefferson's main principle of consent is that those bound most tightly by collective rules must be given the greatest say in the making and enforcing of the rules.

Jefferson stated this idea by writing,

"That which governs the best, governs the least."

In order to install a centralized national government designed to benefit the natural aristocracy, Madison had to start over, with a new constitution.

The centralized power in Madison's rules, originally intended to empower the natural aristocracy, is now in the hands of the Marxist Democrats.

At the time of his convention, in 1787, a small handful of natural rights conservatives were aware of the intent of Madison's scheme, but were too disorganized to defend the nation's first constitution.

Natural rights conservatives, in 1787, had no path of escape from the tyranny imposed by Madison's rules.

Natural rights conservatives, today, have no path of escape from Marxist tyranny, under Madison's rules.

All of the constituent elements to create a new American constitution already exist in the American heritage of the Revolution, along with the spirit of liberty as the guiding ideology for conservatives to follow in replacing Madison's constitution.

In order to install a decentralized national government that enshrines liberty as the national public purpose, natural rights conservatives must start over, with a new constitution, for a new democratic republic of American states.

Chapter 5. New Constitutional Rules for Economic Growth and Financial Stability.

Many conservative Republicans cling to the false hope that, if the current constitution could just be obeyed and the rule of law followed, that the American Ship of State would right itself, for future smooth sailing.

That false hope will not be realized because Madison's unfair rules that elevated the financial interests of the natural aristocracy over common citizens were supplemented by unfair banking and money rules, beginning in 1792, with the creation of the First National Bank.

The First Bank, the Second Bank, and the current Third Bank, The Federal Reserve Bank, all operate outside the authority of the Constitution, with undelegated authority to manage the money and financial affairs of the U. S. Government.

None of the private central banks operated according to some constitutional definition of the public purpose or national mission.

They operate like any other private corporation, to make profits for their shareholders, which are other private banks.

To paraphrase James Buchanan, the welfare that the bankers seek to maximize is their own.

In Buchanan's logical sequence of creating fair constitutional rules, citizens first agree on fair rules for society in the pre-constitutional setting. (The Reason of Rules (with Geoffrey Brennan), 1985.).

Next, after a fair ratification process, citizens agree to obey the rules which they have given to themselves.

In the post-constitutional setting, institutions, such as banks and judicial institutions, are created that are bound to obey the fair constitutional rules.

In Madison's sequence of creating the constitution, rules which benefited the ruling class were first created, in secret, by 38 members of the ruling class.

The creation of the rules violated the provisions of the Articles of Confederation, and the delegates ignored the instructions from their state legislatures to amend the existing constitution.

The rules were never ratified by a vote of the citizens. The rules were ratified in a fraudulent, unconstitutional process, outside the provisions of the Articles of Confederation.

After the fraudulent ratification process, Hamilton created the First National Bank, in 1792, as an institution that empowered the unfair rules for the benefit of the ruling class.

The two components of Madison's process, first the creation of unfair rules, and then the First National Bank, work in tandem.

Reverting back to Madison's rules, even if the Marxist Democrats agreed to obey the rule of law, would not eradicate the unfair judicial and banking institutions, created in the post-constitutional setting.

Hamilton first devised his banking institution, in 1780, based upon his admiration of the Bank of England. His letter to President Washington, in 1791, advocating the creation of the Bank cited his previous report, written in 1780.

We agree with Buchanan that a stable social order would emerge from the operation and transactions that occur in a free market society.

We argue that there is no inherent, structural economic defect in free market exchange, or theoretical explanation, for the economic and financial instability of the American economic history.

The price mechanism of exchange in the market would allow each individual to use the market to obtain future financial prosperity.

The cause of the economic and financial instability in the American economy is the power of the Federal Reserve Bank to manipulate interest rates, increase the supply of money, and promote increased government debt.

That type of private control over the nation's money and fiscal policies leads to a recurring cycle of economic collapse.

The macro economic instability is caused by a predictable sequence of events, beginning with a period of a rapid increase in money supply and an increase in fiscal spending and debt issuance.

The loose money policies cause a period of asset speculation and inflation, designed to benefit the most wealthy families and corporations, who have the financial resources to buy and sell hard assets.

The speculation leads to a gigantic bubble in assets and the creation of synthetic investment instruments, which then burst, causing aggregate economic demand to collapse and asset values to plummet.

In the period of the bubble burst, common citizens lose their houses and their farms to the elite, due to the way the creditor/debtor laws are written to benefit the bankers.

Bankers, and creditors, then proceed to foreclose on the property and assets of common citizens, who cannot make their debt payments.

During the period of asset speculation, the rate of private capital investment collapses, causing economic decline for real productive assets, in the 3 to 5 year horizon, as capital is shifted from productive investments that lead to long-term economic growth to speculative assets in hopes of a short-term capital gain.

One consequence of the control over banking by the elites is that they use the agencies of government and the judicial system to insulate themselves from the damage that they inflict on common citizens.

During the period of economic collapse, the common citizens become financially destitute, and the concentration of wealth, and the distribution of income, becomes more and more concentrated in the hands of the few.

For about the first 200 years of the nation, the banking tyranny by the elites led to economic collapse for common citizens about every 10 years.

In the most recent period of time, the intervals between boom and bust have shortened to around every 5 years.

The nation's banking system collapsed in 1813, as a result of the First Bank's corruption in speculative investments, and the mal-appropriation of Indian lands in Michigan and Ohio.

The banking system, and economy, collapsed again in 1819, as a result of the bank's securities, issued to finance the War of 1812 debt, becoming worthless.

Because European bankers owned securities issued by the First Bank, the 1819 collapse in America's banking system quickly spread to Europe, leading to an international financial collapse.

As a result of the collapse in 1819, the first wave of land appropriation of farm land by the bankers occurred, as farm prices collapsed, and farmers could not pay their debts.

The Tariff of 1824, designed to protect northern financial interests, caused the wholesale price of cotton to drop from 18 cents to 9 cents.

Farmers, in the South, suffered a prolonged depression. The Tariff of '24 marked the first phase of the irreconcilable financial split between northern and southern elites, that culminated in the Civil War.

The U. S. banking system collapsed again, in 1836. As a consequence of this collapse, President Jackson was able to muster enough political support to kill the Second National Bank.

Agricultural land and commodity prices collapsed in 1837, leading to the longest depression in U. S. history.

The 1837 collapse led to the second great wave of land appropriation by the elites, in conjunction with the land appropriation of Indian lands in the middle of the nation, after Jackson forcibly removed the Indians to Oklahoma.

During the financial panic of 1857 the bond notes issued by 1400 state banks became worthless. During this collapse, 5000 businesses failed, leading to the first wave of massive unemployment of common workers in U. S. metro regions, just prior to the start of the Civil War.

In the aftermath of the Civil War, the economy of the south was in a state of economic depression for 50 years. One consequence of that depression was that thousands of farmers lost their lands in the debt-peonage system, and were forced to work in the textile and tobacco industry, in an economic system called "neo-slavery."

In his book, The Mind of the South, C. Wright Mills correctly described this era as the re-establishment of the Plantation Aristocracy in the mills, achieved by brute force and racial apartheid.

The 175 year period of economic instability in America changed in 1964, with the shift in political power to global corporations, who exerted power in Washington with the agents of the nascent military-industrial deep state.

Beginning with the 1987 stock market collapse, the cycle of economic instability became more frequent, and more intense.

As the corporations extended their crony capitalist political power, they were successful in implementing tax and trade policies skewed to their benefit.

Between 1985 and 1992, changes in tax and trade policies led to increased rates of manufacturing and production jobs lost due to offshoring and outsourcing.

On October 19, 1987, the Black Monday Stock Market Crash occurred. The cause of the crash was banking collusion with agents of the deep state, asset speculation, insider trading and program trading by 5 large global securities firms.

In 1991, the speculative real estate bubble, and the leveraged buy-out bubble, both burst at the same time, causing the recession of 1991.

The capital gains and profits from the exits in IT investments, initially made in 1992, were ploughed back into short-term speculative early stage IPO investments, in 1997.

Speculation and collusion in the IPO market dumped hundreds of millions of worthless IT securities into the public markets for ordinary American investors to buy.

The government intervention and increased spending, in 2001, did not create lasting benefits because domestic markets and the global economy were no longer integrated.

The economic multiplier effects of increased government spending primarily occurred in overseas economies, not the U. S. domestic economy.

After the Islamic terrorist attack, on September 11, 2001, the US. stock market collapsed again. The U. S. economy entered a prolonged recession.

Again, the U. S. government, and the Federal Reserve Bank, tried stimulus spending, which ended up primarily benefitting special financial interests in foreign counties and domestic real estate speculation in the U. S.

In 2002, U. S. trade and tax policies were changed to facilitate more offshoring of technology innovation and R&D. The primary beneficiary of the new trade polices was China, admitted to the World Trade Organization, as an undeveloped nation.

The changes in regulation of corporations led to a series of Enron-type collapses and wide-spread corporate financial accounting fraud.

In the period from 2003 to 2008, the U. S. rate of job creation was lower than the rate of job destruction.

Beginning in 2003, the U. S. rate of domestic direct investment declined, and U. S. foreign direct investment increased, primarily in China and India.

In 2004, as a result of the New World Order trade policies, the U. S. rates of corporate profit for the 1500 largest global corporation increased to record levels.

As a result of U. S. trade and tax policies, those record profits were not repatriated, or reinvested, in U. S. domestic value chains. The record profits were reinvested in foreign global value chains, primarily in China.

The trade policies and increased foreign capital investment had created a bifurcated domestic economy. A large part of the domestic economy, about 75% of GDP, were not connected to global value chains, and did not benefit from transactions in the global corporate value chains.

A large part of the U. S. domestic economy transitioned from manufacturing to 7 service sectors, with about 80% of the domestic labor force working in hotels, restaurants, and hair salons.

As a consequence of losing domestic manufacturing, the U. S. domestic economy also lost the ability to generate technology innovation, which occurs in the intermediate domestic value chains, that were now located in India and China.

Beginning in March, 2008, speculation in oil and gas increased the price of a barrel of oil from $43 per barrel to $145 per barrel. The asset speculation was a result of collusion between oil corporations and government officials, aided and abetted by a useless war in Iraq and Afghanistan.

The rapid increase in oil prices caused a sharp contraction in consumer spending. The decreased consumer spending caused a prolonged economic recession.

In September 2008, the mortgage debt asset bubble, directly caused by U. S. government banking and interest rate policies, burst, and the U. S. economy collapsed again.

As a result of that collapse, and coincident with the election of a socialist president, the U. S. economy did not experience growth for the next 8 years.

In response to the 2008 economic collapse, the Fed manipulated interest rates to near zero, and pumped up the rate of money increase, at the same time that U. S. long term debt exploded.

Recently, around 2022, the Fed jerked interest rates higher. Current 30-year mortgages are around 8%, designed to burst the real estate asset bubble.

Madison's centralized constitutional power, in conjunction with Hamilton's central banking powers, evolved into a modern era ruling class driven global economy, dominated by wealthy families in the American ruling class, large corporations and global central bankers, primarily the Bank of England.

Hamilton created the First Bank as a private-for-profit corporation, that was not subject to state taxes, under the provisions of the Congressional Charter that established the First Bank as the banker for the new government.

As a private corporation, the contracts and activities of the Bank were protected from interference, by either the states or the federal government, by the Contracts Clause.

Madison inserted the Contracts Clause towards the end of the Convention, so that a State would not be allowed to pass any law that "impairs the obligation of contracts."

Inserting the contracts clause represents one of Madison's most clandestine acts in preserving the validity of slave contracts for the Southern slaveocracy,.

As a compliment to the Contracts Clause in solidifying the balance of power, Supreme Court Justice Marshall ruled that the Federal government, under the necessary and proper clause, could create any type of financial corporation that could possibly be seen to promote the "general welfare."

Hamilton wrote to President Washington, in 1791,

"Every power vested in Government is in its nature sovereign and includes by force of the term a right to employ all means requisite and fairly applicable to the attainment of such power."

Twenty years later, Justice Marshall, in his ruling on McCullough vs. Maryland (1819), re-stated Hamilton's words, almost verbatim,

"Let the end be legitimate, let it be within the scope of the constitution, and all means which are appropriate are constitutional."

In conjunction with the Contracts Clause, Madison's constitution prohibited states from issuing their own paper money and from regulating the banking affairs of the central government.

The Constitution defines bills of credit to signify a paper medium of exchange intended to circulate, like money, between individuals, and between the Government and individuals, for the ordinary purposes of economic transactions.

States previously issued bills of credit to pay for government expenses. The Constitution forbid states from issuing bills of credit because they were not "legal tender," as defined by the Constitution.

As a part of cementing the privileges of the natural aristocracy, Justice Marshall ruled that when, and where, either the state, or Federal government, received state bank notes in payment and discharge of an execution, (Contracts Clause), the creditor (natural aristocracy), was entitled to demand payment in gold or silver, (Commerce Clause).

The pathway of corporations to become "persons" under the 14th Amendment, is almost as fraudulent and illegitimate as the so-called ratification process of Madison's constitution.

Becoming a person allowed corporations to assume the same legal rights of natural persons, with increased legal authority to use the 14th amendment to extend their political power.

We rely on Adam Winkler's article "Corporations Are People' Is Built on an Incredible 19th-Century Lie: How a farcical series of events in the 1880s produced an enduring and controversial legal precedent." (The Atlantic, 2018.), to make our case about the illegitimate rulings that made corporations "persons."

The judicial farce of granting banks and corporations the same natural rights as natural persons, began in 1882, and, according to Winkler, the farce,

"Involved a lawyer who lied to the Supreme Court, an ethically challenged justice, [a corrupt court recorder who modified the text of the opinion] and one of the most powerful corporations of the day." [a railroad].

The corrupt attorney, who lied to the Supreme Court, represented the Southern Pacific Railroad. Roscoe Conkling had been a member of Congress, and served on the committee that drafted the text of the 14th Amendment [in 1868].

Conkling both represented the railroad in the case before the Supreme Court, and also provided direct testimony, and introduced evidence, based upon his work in drafting the 14th Amendment.

According to Winkler,

"The head lawyer representing Southern Pacific was a man named Roscoe Conkling. Conkling told the justices that the drafters had changed the wording of the amendment, replacing "citizens" with "persons" in order to cover corporations too. Laws referring to "persons," he said, have "by long and constant acceptance … been held to embrace artificial persons as well as natural persons." Conkling buttressed his account with a surprising piece of evidence: a musty old journal he claimed was a previously unpublished record of the deliberations of the drafting committee. [that Conkling stated supported his contention about changing the word "citizens" to the word "persons"] . According to historians, Conkling was simply lying.

Nonetheless, the Supreme Court embraced Conkling's reading of the Fourteenth Amendment."

The corrupt court reporter modified the text of the opinion, and added his revised rendition at the top of the Court's ruling. Davis was also an attorney and had represented railroads, before he became a Supreme Court recorder.

According to Winkler,

"By tradition, the reporter writes up a summary of the Court's opinion and includes it at the beginning of the opinion. The reporter in the 1880s was J. C. Bancroft Davis, whose wildly inaccurate summary of the Southern Pacific case said that the Court had ruled that "corporations are persons within ... the Fourteenth Amendment."

The corrupt Supreme Court Justice was Stephen Johnson Field. According to Winkler, Field used the fraudulent document, prepared by the Court recorder, as legal precedent to be followed by subsequent Courts.

"A few years later, in an opinion in an unrelated case, Field wrote that "corporations are persons within the meaning" of the Fourteenth Amendment. "It was so held in Santa Clara County v. Southern Pacific Railroad," explained Field, who knew very well that the Court had done no such thing." [Field had prior knowledge of Conklin's strategy and knew at the time, in 1882, that Conkling was lying to the Court].

In 1886, in Santa Clara County v. Southern Pacific Rail Road, the Court cited the legal precedent, established by Field, in an unrelated case, that corporations were "persons" under the 14th Amendment.

In the 1886 case, Chief Justice Morrison Waite, stated,

"The Court does not wish to hear an argument on the question whether the provision in the Fourteenth Amendment to the Constitution which forbids a state to deny to any person within its jurisdiction the equal protection of the laws applies to these corporations. We are all of opinion that it does…The defendant Corporations are persons within the intent of the clause in section 1 of the Fourteenth Amendment to the Constitution of the United States, which forbids a state to deny to any person within its jurisdiction the equal protection of the laws."

Winkler concludes his article by noting that the 14th Amendment, purportedly passed to protect the civil rights of Black people, had instead been turned into a political weapon to protect the civil rights of corporations.

He writes,

"Between 1868, when the 14th amendment was ratified, and 1912, the Supreme Court would rule on 28 cases involving the rights of African Americans and an astonishing 312 cases [affirming] the rights of corporations."

As we argued above about the logic of reverting back to Madison's constitution, the Supreme Court decision defining corporations as a person would not revoke this unfair power of corporations.

Corporations and banks are not the same legal entities as persons, and the illogical definition of corporations as persons, and the illegitimate power of the Federal Reserve, must be replaced by a new constitution that enshrines liberty as the mission of the new nation.

During the period of time, from 1882 to the creation of the Federal Reserve Act, in 1913, U. S. corporations began the transition from a national monopoly power to a global imperial power, fueled by their new domestic monopoly power legal rights.

As described by James Livingston, in Origins of the Federal Reserve System, Money, Class, and Corporate Capitalism, 1890-1913., (1986), the transition to a global imperial power required a new, and different type of banking system, than the "free banking" system that existed during the Gilded Age.

He writes,

"The federal reserve system was a product of the crisis of the 1890s…the market investment [banking] system was reorganized and stabilized…The banking and monetary reform movement of 1894 must be understood as the context in which a corporate business elite began to work on [creating] a world view and a program appropriate to its control over an emergent modern industrial society."

The Fed adds to (or subtracts from) the amount of money in the economy by buying (or selling) U.S. Treasury securities and other financial instruments. This is referred to as "open market operations," since these transactions take place in the open market.

The Fed pays for those securities by crediting funds to the reserves that banks are required to hold, either cash in their vaults or deposits at a Reserve bank.

The Fed's computerized crediting of new reserves for banks is just like the ACH checking account transfers for ordinary citizens.

One day the checking account of a bank is empty. The next day, after the Fed's ACH transfer, the checking account of the bank has millions of dollars.

It is just like the Fed creating money out of thin air.

But, what the Fed giveth, the Fed can easily take away, by changing the overnight reserve requirements for commercial banks.

The website, The Last Refuge, has been offering a concise economic explanation of the recent American economic collapse, for the economic period, beginning with the end of the Soviet Union, in 1990, the entrance of China into the World Trade Organization in 2001, up to the 2022 economic collapse.

Much of his explanation of the current American economic collapse revolves around the deliberate, coordinated actions of the world's central bankers in manipulating the money supply, currency exchange rates, and interest rates to bring about a global economic collapse.

The main point is that the central bankers of the New World Order engineered a global energy crisis to conform energy production to the previous supply levels 50 years ago, and their shortage of energy supply precipitated a global economic collapse, in conjunction with rapid M2 money creation and government spending, which precipitated global inflation.

During the plunder and investment speculation phase of the U. S. economy, the Board of Governors are directly responsible for causing the economic conditions of inflation and easy credit by their manipulation of interest rates and bank reserve requirements.

After each collapse, the Board of Governors act to restore the banks and corporations to their former economic social status by bailing them out.

The Fed's rules result in a cycle of corruption and speculation, which results in economic collapse, not real, sustained, economic growth.

The political propaganda in support of the Federal Reserve cites its role in stabilizing the economy, especially during the periods of aggregated demand collapse.

In contrast, we argue that price and monetary stability, in the American economy, can never be achieved by financial elites at the Federal Reserve Bank because central planned economies are not as socially stable as the price-based outcomes derived by the free market exchange.

By constantly manipulating both the money supply and interest rates in the belief that they know more than millions of people, the Fed, and the two predecessor national banks, has created tremendous economic instability.

If the U. S. economy were ever set free of the constant money and interest rate manipulation of the Fed, the national economy would experience unprecedented economic stability and prosperity.

In contrast to this ruling class propaganda about the benefits of the Fed, we cite Buchanan's concept of creating constitutional rules would lead to an institutional stable social order, based upon voluntary citizen cooperation.

Buchanan explained that every set of constitutional rules has an internal end-goal to which the rules are directed.

In Logical Foundations of Constitutional Liberty, (1999), Buchanan relies on a philosophy of logic to explain how the end goals of a constitution, clearly stated in the preamble, create the binding allegiance of citizens to follow the rule of law.

Buchanan states,

"Uncertainty about just where one's own interest will lie in a sequence of plays or rounds will lead a rational person, from his own interest, to prefer rules and arrangements, or constitutions that will seem fair, no matter what final positions he might occupy."

His first principle of logic is that all individuals are rational in the pursuit of their own sovereign life mission,

In The Theory of Public Choice, (1972), he defines an individual not so much from the perspective of insight-imagination, but from the brain's rational choice attribute.

He states that,

"…we can simply define a person in terms of his set of preferences, his utility function. This function defines or describes a set of possible trade-offs among alternatives for potential choice."

In The Reason of Rules. Buchanan explains the importance of how citizens provide prior consent to follow the rules that they give to themselves.

"Just conduct," writes Buchanan, "consists of behavior that does not violate rules to which one has given prior consent."

In other words, rather than relying on the separation of powers to deal with the problem of special interests, as Madison did, Buchanan relies upon the rationality of self-interest as a force that binds individuals to society as a process of rationally minimizing risk in uncertain decision making environments.

In leaving the state of nature, and forming a constitution, Buchanan explains, individuals are placed in a position of uncertainty in the outcome of their life's mission.

No individual knows in advance where the individual may end up, given the choice between one set of constitutional rules or another.

His logic of individual rationality is that any individual, with a rational self-interest, would choose fair rules for all, aimed at the greatest freedom for all.

In constitutional decision-making under uncertainty, individuals would seek rules that had maximum equal rights for all, with special privileges for none.

The end goal, or telos, of the constitution, in this case of rational self-interest, is individual liberty.

Buchanan wrote,

"To the extent that Madison's constitution commands little respect, it is, in part, because it fails in its function of limiting the scope of both governmental and private intrusion into what are widely held to be protected spheres of activity."

In The Reason of Rules, Buchanan and Brennan write,

"Our specific claim is that justice takes its meaning from the rules for the social order within which notions of justice are to be applied. To appeal to considerations of justice is to appeal to relevant rules. These rules provide the framework within which patterns of distributional end states emerge from the interaction of persons who play various complex functional roles."

In other words, fair distribution of income and wealth, under Buchanan, is obtained through just rules of financial and economic exchange.

Buchanan's interpretation of justice as fair rules is dramatically different than Madison's rules of civil procedure.

Buchanan applies his concept of justice to his suggestions about the relationship between free markets and governmental power.

He states that,

"…for most persons, the independence offered by the presence of market alternatives offers the maximal liberty possible. But we have not yet designed institutions that will satisfy the individual's search for community in the impersonal setting of the market order without, at the same time, undermining the very independence that this order afford."

We argue that there is only one configuration of constitutional rules, and only one method of citizen participation in the making of fair constitutional rules, that creates maximum rates of economic growth, and maximum diffusion of income benefits to all social classes of citizens.

That single constitutional configuration creates the maximum level of trust among citizens, so that citizens can trust each other to obey the rule of law.

Buchanan's constitution aims at the creation of rules, in the pre-constitutional setting, that limits the power of government to exclusively providing the functions of property-rights protection and public-goods provision, without overstepping its limits into civil rights predation or wealth redistribution.

Brennan and Buchanan's remedy for Madison's open-ended special interest tyranny relies on the potential for changes in the pre-constitutional rule making and post constitutional political rules that constrains the power of the central government.

"These [pre-constitutional] rules provide the framework within which [the post-constitutional institutional] patterns of distributional end states emerge from the interaction of persons who play various complex functional [market and political] roles."

In other words, Buchanan's constitution would severely limit the central government's range of power so that citizen free choice in subsequent market and political institutions would allow a stable social order to emerge.

Buchanan states that economic growth and social prosperity arise from the economic market institutions that allow for voluntary exchange to take place, in the post-constitutional setting.

The lynchpin that binds citizen allegiance to obey the rule of law is future economic growth, in which all citizens have an equal opportunity to benefit.

The only unambiguous goal of public economic policy is private sector economic growth, caused by private capital market investments.

We argue that in the new constitution the goal of economic growth replaces the current goal of a target rate of inflation.

In other words, the linkage between citizen allegiance to the rule of law in pre-constitutional fair rules and post-constitutional fair institutions is future economic growth.

Peter J. Boettke and Christopher J. Coyne describe the relative importance between the function of economic growth, and constitutionally protected individual liberty.

They state,

"The connection [Buchanan sees between free market exchange and individual liberty] begins with his individualistic approach to economics. Individuals have their own goals and desires, and the purpose of economic activity is to enable them to cooperate with each other so they can further those goals. As economists depict it, individuals have "utility functions" and they make choices that enable them to maximize their utility [wealth]. What this means in more common language is that individuals have their own goals, which each individual understands better than does anyone else. And the subject of economics, as Buchanan saw it, is to analyze how individuals interact for their mutual benefit in furtherance of those goals…The distribution of product among social classes [welfare redistribution] is clearly secondary to production…[economic growth]. [Economic growth occurs] by the removal of government constraints on individual liberty." (Boettke, Peter J. and Coyne, Christopher J., Methodological Individualism, Spontaneous Order and the Research Program of the Workshop in Political Theory and Policy Analysis, George Mason University, Department of Economics, 2004.).

Buchanan contends that the standard rule for the monetary policy of the nation is,

"Predictability in the value of the monetary unit, or, reciprocally, in the absolute level of prices." Importantly, this criterion [of future predictability] differs from monetary stability…monetary stability is plagued with vagueness. Predictability, especially with reference to the general level of prices, is free from that difficulty Furthermore, predictability, by maintaining "continuous monetary equilibrium" would entail real efficiency gains: by enshrining, in the form of a [binding constitutional] rule, the purchasing power of the monetary unit, economic actors would better be able to coordinate their activities, resulting in further exhaustion of the gains from trade than would otherwise exist… institutions of private [free market exchange] decision-making in such a way that the desired monetary predictability will emerge spontaneously from the ordinary operations of the system…Unconstrained government monopoly in money creation cannot emerge from a genuine constitutional calculus, The argument for a monetary constitution is an argument for true rules, which actually bind monetary policy decision makers." (Buchanan, 1962.).

The standard of value for money, as a medium of exchange, is the rate of economic growth of the national gross domestic product, not some fixed value of a commodity, like bricks or gold.

Buchanan affirms that the rule for increasing the money supply must be limited by constitutional barriers.

"In application to money, the requirement is that the value of the monetary unit be made one of the rules of the game, within which economic interaction takes place, rather than being used as a counter in the strategy of play within the rules. In Hayekian parlance, the value of money must be part of the 'higher law,' as opposed to ordinary legislation that takes place within such law." (Buchanan, James M., The Limits of Liberty: Between Anarchy and Leviathan, University of Chicago Press, 1975.).

Monetary policy, tax systems, tax rates, and limits on government spending and debt, would all be included as components under the pre-constitutional setting in the new constitution that replaces Madison's constitution.

In the post-constitutional institutional setting, the agencies of the national government, and elected representatives, would be bound by rules on increasing taxation linked to clear sources of revenue, to tax systems with uniform rates on the allowed tax bases, and ideally to tax bases that are complementary to the public services desired.

We offer four new components of the new constitution which replaces Madison's constitution.

All four components seek to eliminate the discretionary power of the current Fed which operates to benefit the ruling class, in order to re-direct the mission of the future national bank to attaining high rates of domestic private capital investment for the benefit of working class and middle class common citizens.

1. A constitutionally-mandated balanced budget provision.
2. A constitutionally-mandated provision on national tax increases, that is ratified by a majority of state legislatures.
3. A constitutional limit on the issuance of national government debt, linked to the rate of increase in national GDP.
4. A constitutional mechanism that allows interest rates to be established by private capital markets in a future exchange marketplace.

The specific text of these proposed components of the new constitution do not currently exist, but would be defined in the pre-constitutional setting of state legislatures.

In the most general form, the balanced budget provision would require that "total outlays shall not exceed total receipts for a fiscal period," generally a two year budget cycle.

Again, in the most general form, the balanced budget provision would be linked to text on tax increases, which would first be adopted by a majority vote in the new lower chamber, and would require approval by 60% of the state legislatures that voted to be a part of the new constitution.

The increase of national debt by issuance of 10-year government bonds would place a constitutional limit on the amount of new debt for all gross public debt, including debt held in the future government's own trust accounts.

The maximum issuance of new debt in any fiscal period would be constitutionally limited by the gross national debt, linked to a percentage of the national GDP in a two year budget cycle.

The current Fed's ability to manipulate interest rates would be eliminated and replaced by private capital market transactions, in a yet-to-be developed future interest rate exchange, that would function much like the existing futures exchanges in the Chicago Mercantile Exchange.

As a way of promoting discussion and debate, we offer the following text to begin the pre-constituional dialogue.

The National Congress will operate the Democratic Republic of America according to a balanced budget, during a budget cycle of two years, where the expenditures of the Government do not exceed the tax revenues set to meet those expenditures.

The National Government budget, and all bills for raising revenue, shall originate in the Senate, to be completed no later than the day before the August adjournment.

Every budget bill which shall have passed the Senate shall be transmitted to the House. The House must vote on the proposed budget of the Senate by November 30, of each year, or the national budget will revert to the same budget as the previous 2 years.

A budget passed by the House, and the proposed rate of taxes to meet the budget, must be presented to the President of the Democratic Republic of America on December 1, to approve or reject, by December 20 of each year. Upon a rejection by the President, the budget reverts to the same budget as the previous 2 years.

The National Congress shall have power to lay and collect taxes, duties, imposts and excises, to meet the expenditures of the 2 year balanced budget. All duties, imposts and excises shall be uniform throughout the Democratic Republic of America.

No tax or duty shall be laid on articles exported from any state to another state.

No State shall enter into any trade treaty, or trade alliance with a foreign nation.

The National Congress shall have the power to issue government bonds, and to borrow money on the credit of the Democratic Republic of America. All proposals to borrow money or issue debt shall occur once in the two year budget cycle, and all proposals to issue debt must be approved by 50% of the State legislatures of the Democratic Republic of America, no later than January 21 of the year of issuance.

The term of debt and interest on any issuance of debt shall not exceed 10 years, and must be paid in full by the end of the 10th year.

Chapter 6. Establishing The Public Purpose of National Economic Sovereignty In A New Constitution.

Madison's constitution contained a fatal defect for protecting the national economic sovereignty of the United States because his rules were "designed" to handle the problem of an unjust and overpowering majority of common citizens using the government to oppress the property rights of the minority natural aristocracy.

His constitution was not designed to promote the financial interests of the majority of common citizens through rules of market exchange for a competitive free market economy where common citizens had an equal opportunity to obtain wealth and prosperity.

The defect continues to create a threat to liberty because the financial interests of the new American ruling class are disconnected from the will of the people, and Madison's constitution contains no mechanism for common citizens to re-establish the consent of the governed.

The government, in the hands of the ruling class, has a will of its own, and that will serves the interests of large global corporations, who seek to bend the flow of income from the global value chains to themselves.

In Locke's language of a social contract, the global corporations domiciled in the U. S. extract advantages and benefits in global trade and currency supremacy from the government, without providing an equivalent fair exchange of value to the majority of middle class citizens who live in the U.S.

In Buchanan's fair rules of making a constitution, the common citizens in America would never have voluntarily agreed to be governed by these unfair rules.

Madison's defect of leaving the national public economic purpose out of the Preamble caused exactly the reverse type of tyranny that Madison feared.

Instead of a common citizen majority who use government to extract benefits from the ruling class, Madison's rules evolved into a privileged minority of wealthy elites and corporations who use the agencies of government to obtain special privileges and corporate welfare in the crony capitalist system.

We argue that reverting to Madison's constitution, today, even if the Democrat Marxists pledged allegiance to obey the rule of law, will not resolve the Constitution's absence of national economic sovereignty in the evolution of the United States economy to a global corporatist world economy.

The national economic sovereignty is diminished by the unelected political power of the global corporations, in the operation of the crony capitalist plunder system, combined with the open border policies of the social justice ideology of the Democrat Marxist in their quest for a one-world global Marxist state.

Madison's defect originates in his initial assumptions and theory of government, which are based upon his admiration of the British constitution that serves as a model for his American version of government.

His application of the British model of government contains four major flaws as applied to the American society.

- Society is comprised of two social classes which are in eternal conflict over the distribution of income and wealth.
- One of the social classes possesses intelligence and virtue, which makes the decisions of that social class superior to the decisions of the other social class in creating the conditions for social order.
- The inferior decisions of the lower social class, in a representative republic, can be ameliorated by diluting their political influence over an extended republic to foreclose the possibility that the lower social class would form a social class consciousness,

as the common citizens in England had already developed.
- The public purpose, or constitutional national mission can be discerned by the natural aristocracy, and the authority for making decisions is, by right and ought, to be placed, forever, in the hands of the natural aristocracy.

The original grant of constitutional authority in Madison's rules, intended to empower the natural aristocracy over the common citizens, transitioned to an unchecked and undemocratic power of global corporations who seek a new world order that eliminates the sovereignty of the United States.

Madison saw the American society as comprised of two social classes, creditors and debtors, who were in eternal economic conflict with each other..

In his conception of the rules of society, the two social classes are a permanent feature of all human societies, throughout all human history.

According to Michael Zuckert,

"Madison's conflict was expressed as the natural property rights of creditors versus the political rights of debtors, where the natural property rights are superior to the political rights that are derived from the higher status of property rights. Madison protected the minority rights of creditors against the majority rights of debtors." (Zuckert, Michael, The Natural Rights Republic: Studies In The Foundation of The American Political Tradition, 1996.).

In "The Constitutional Convention of 1787: A Biographical Dictionary," Joseph C. Morton, writes about the social class unity of the natural aristocracy in Madison's day.

He writes,

"[The aristocracy was] from the uppermost economic, political, and social strata of American society…they were an exceedingly homogeneous group regarding most economic, social and political matters." (2006.).

From Madison's conception of human nature, there is little that can, or should be done, to eliminate the factions, or social class conflict, between the two social classes.

In Madison's conception of society, the upper class has known and scientifically objective characteristics of virtue, and the lower class has known and objective characteristics of fermenting social disorder.

Madison states in Federalist #10,

"They [the common citizens] will introduce "instability, injustice and confusion" into our highest councils and when the opportunity presents itself—once, that is, they are the "superior force" —they will rule without regard for the "rules of justice and the [property] rights of the minor party. [natural aristocracy.]."

Madison had stated, early in the Convention, that his intent was to divide the society into two distinct social classes, to the benefit of the natural aristocracy.

Before he left the Convention in disgust, in June of 1787, at the plan being proposed by Madison, Robert Yates took notes on what Madison said.

From Robert Yates' notes on Madison's statement of intent,

[Quoting] Mr. Madison. We are now to determine whether the republican form shall be the basis of our government. I admit there is weight in objection of the gentleman from South Carolina [Pinckney]; but the plan can steer clear of objections. That great powers [of the cental government] are to be gained, there is no doubt; and that those powers may be abused is equally true. It is also probable that members may lose their attachment the states which sent them. Yet the first branch [Senate] Will control the many [common citizens] of their abuses. But we are now forming a body on the wisdom [of the natural aristocracy] we mean to rely, and their permanency in office secured in proper field which they may exert their firmness and knowledge. Democratic communities may be unsteady, and be led to action by impulse of the moment. Like individuals they may be sensible in their own [financial] decisions. They [common citizens] have Weakness, and may desire the counsels to guard them against the turbulency and weakness of their passions. Such are the various pursuits of this life, that in all Civil countries, the interest of a community will be divided. There will debtors and creditors, and an unequal possession of property, hence arises different views and different objects in government. indeed is the groundwork of aristocracy; and we find it blends into every government, both ancient and modem. Even where titles survived property, we discover the noble beggar haughtily assuming an equal status." (Slonim,Shlomo, Framers' Construction/Beardian Deconstruction" Essays on the Constitutional Design of 1787. 2001.).

On June 19, 1787, early in the deliberations of the Convention, Alexander Hamilton expressed the social class conflict perspective that the ruling class used as the reasons for calling the Convention to overthrow the Articles of Confederation.

Hamilton stated,

"All communities divide themselves into the few and the many. The first are the rich and wellborn, the other the mass of the people…The people are turbulent and changing; they seldom judge or determine right. Give therefore to the first class a distinct, permanent share in the government. They will check the unsteadiness of the second, and as they cannot receive any advantage by a change, they therefore will ever maintain good government."

According to Madison and Hamilton, the best idea to preserve social order, was to place the powers of the central government permanently in the hands of the virtuous ruling class.

While Madison mentions multiple conflicting factions in his theory of the extended republic, his theory contains only two social classes, the natural aristocracy and common citizens.

Madison's goal of the extended republic was to eliminate the threat of the common citizens in America that he saw in the unified social class ideology of common citizens in England.

In the logic of Madison's extended republic, the common citizens would never develop a social class ideology that would disrupt the agenda of the ruling class if the common citizen's class interests were dispersed across the extended republic.

In Madison's theory of the extended republic, after elected common citizen representatives from outside of Washington arrived in the Capital, their agenda would be controlled by the dominant ideology of the ruling class in the Senate and Supreme Court.

Jacob Levy cites Jefferson as pointing out the logical flaw in Madison's rules regarding the extended republic.

Quoting Jefferson,

"Large republics could better protect freedom than a small one, but only if, and in part, because of it was organized with both separation of powers and federalism. [state sovereignty] When all government, domestic and foreign, in little as in great things, shall be drawn to Washington as the center of all power, it will render powerless the checks and balances provided one government on another, and will become as venal and oppressive as the government from which we separated. [England]. (Levy, Jacob T., Beyond Publius: Montesquieu, Liberal Republicanism and the Small-Republic Thesis, JSTOR, 2006.).

What Jefferson meant was that when the geographically dispersed common citizen representatives arrive in Washington, they would engage in the ideology of shared plunder of the natural aristocracy, and not the defense of individual liberty because they have no class awareness of their own class interests in political equality.

Madison's extended republic ensured that the common citizens would never form a social class consciousness of their own financial interests that may compete with the existing well-organized ruling class faction, which saw themselves as a unified social class.

Madison wrote in Federalist #10, that in the extended republic, it will be difficult for common citizens to form a coherent social class ideology.

He wrote,

"The interests and parties [of the common citizens] will be so numerous that it will be difficult for them to discover a common motive [social class ideology] for oppressive action. [against the natural aristocracy]. And even if such a motive does exist it will be more difficult for all who feel it [social class ideology] to discover their own strength, and to act in unison with each other."

Madison wrote in Federalist #57, that in the extended republic, it was less likely that common citizens would engage as effectively in plunder and corruption as the natural aristocracy, or the

"intrigues of the ambitious, or the bribes of the rich"

In contrast to common citizens, the ruling class had, according to Madison, both virtue and love of justice,

"whose patriotism and love of justice will be least likely to sacrifice the common good to temporary or partial considerations."

Kaminsky and Leffler cite the natural rights patriot, Cato, in his opposition to Madison's logic of the extended republic.

"[The common citizen representatives from the extended republic will be] composed of interests opposite and dissimilar in their nature, and [the government] will in its exercise emphatically be like a house divided against itself by indispensibly placing trust in the hands of individuals whose ambitions for power and agrandisement will oppress and grind you." [after they get to Washington]. (Kaminski, John P., and Leffler, Richard, Federalists and Antifederalists: The Debate Over the Ratification of the Constitution. 1998.).

The elites had a common social class background and a unified ideology of the aristocracy, which guided them in the creation of the rules of the constitution.

The unified and coherent social class awareness of the aristocracy in America was based upon the shared understanding that it was their social class financial connections to the British aristocracy that had rewarded their financial interests.

In order to preserve their social class privileges, Madison intended to replicate the British social class conflict model in America.

Merrill Jensen quotes Gouverneur Morris, a delegate from New York, who wrote, in 1774,

"That the British connection was the guarantee of the existing aristocratic order"

In Jensen's book, he writes that,

" after the revolution, they [the aristocrats] engaged with conservatives [elites] in other states in undoing the Articles of Confederation." (Jensen, Merrill, The Articles of Confederation. 1970.).

William Domhoff cites the importance of social class awareness among members of the ruling class in maintaining social and political control.

His term for their power is "class dominance."

He writes,

"Involvement in these institutions usually instills a class consciousness that includes feelings of superiority, pride, and justified privilege. Deep down, most members of the upper class think they are better than other people and therefore fully deserving of their station in life—an attitude that is very useful in managing employees, even though it is sometimes psychologically debilitating. This class consciousness is ultimately based in the society-wide categories of owners and nonowners, but it is reinforced by the shared social identities and interpersonal ties created by participation in social institutions of the upper class." (Who Rules America, Power, Politics, & Social Change. 2021.).

The dominant ideology of the ruling class was their belief in their entitlement to rule, and their social class privilege of shared plunder of social and economic assets.

The common citizens did not have a coherent ideology of liberty, and were locked out of attending the Convention.

The new government was not "of the people," it was government of the natural aristocracy, who obtained their very own unelected branch of government, called the Senate, and an unelected permanently superior ruling class power of the U. S. Supreme Court to determine the constitutional meaning of the public purpose.

Madison knew at the time that he secretly changed the wording in the Preamble, in the last days of the Convention, to "We, the people," from "We. The people of the 13 states," that it was a false statement designed to deceive common citizens.

In the theory of the extended republic, the two parties to Madison's constitutional contract were a collectivist, synthetic imaginary definition of the entire society, "We, the people," and a powerful centralized government in the hands of the natural aristocracy.

In reality, the two parties to the contract were a unified natural aristocracy, and the nascent government, whose rules they created.

"We, the people," was, in reality, the 38 elites who signed the document, as if they were "We, the people."

The consequence of the ideology of shared plunder, today, is that the government and the lobbyists in Washington have a will of their own, independent of the will of the common citizens.

Madison did not define the public purpose or common mission of national economic sovereignty in the Preamble because he assumed that the natural aristocracy could define the national purpose, after they arrived in Washington.

Madison assumed that the natural aristocracy of the Supreme Court, and the federal law as the supreme law of the land, could make up the public purpose as they went along in time, because those decisions would permanently be placed in the hands of the virtuous ruling class.

This assumption was the primary reason why Madison argued that the constitution did not need a Bill of Rights, because the rules in the constitution, in the hands of the ruling class, were sufficient, by themselves, for the elite to define natural rights, for all of time.

The so-called common good was whatever the ruling class elites determined it to be, or in the modern version, whatever 5 Supreme Court justices decide it to be, because Madison's Preamble failed to define the constitutional public purpose.

Madison wrote in Federalist #10, that the natural aristocracy would define what was in the best interests of common citizens better than the common citizens themselves.

"[The natural aristocracy was] a group of decision-makers sufficiently detached from the immediate interests of a given controversy that they would serve more or less as a jury to judge the relative merits of the arguments and proposals advanced by the interested and contending parties. The members of the independent force would necessarily change from issue to issue as different interests become embroiled in controversy. Yet, the point is that on any given issue the force would be of sufficient size to hold the balance among contending interests [to determine what the public ipurpose is]… [the elite] would refine and enlarge the public view and whose wisdom may best discern the true interest of the country.[public purpose] the representatives of the people, [ruling class] will be more consonant to the public good than if pronounced by the people themselves, convened for the purpose."

Madison continues arguing his logic of the national public purpose, in Federalist #10,

"it may well happen that the public voice, pronounced by the representatives of the people, will be more consonant to the public good [as defined by the natural aristocracy] than if pronounced by the people themselves, convened for the purpose…The representative assembly, for one thing, will constitute a "chosen body of citizens" that will "refine and enlarge the public view" and "whose wisdom may best discern the true interest of the country."

The "true interests" of the country are left undefined in Madison's Preamble because Madison falsely assumed that the true interests of the nation would always be the exclusive property and financial interests of the ruling class.

In the evolution of the American economy from one of domestic economic sovereignty to a globalist crony capitalist economy, those property and financial interests transferred to the global corporations.

Eventually, the flaws in Madison's rules allowed the corporate and financial elite to disconnect their government welfare benefits from the consent of the governed.

Madison's defect continues to prohibit common citizens from re-asserting the concept of self-government based upon the consent of the governed because Madison's constitution deliberately left their financial interests unprotected in his rules from the newly emerged political system of global crony capitalism.

For Madison, the supreme sovereign value of the nation resided in the social order that could be obtained by rule of the virtuous natural aristocracy.

The sovereignty of the nation of the United States was based in Madison's belief that the natural aristocracy had a divine right to rule in the same way that the monarch in England had a divine right to rule.

In answer to the question raised by Hobbes of what social force would replace the King or the Pope to insure social stability, Madison answered that the natural aristocracy replaced the king.

Locke, Mason, and Jefferson proposed that sovereignty resided in the citizen's right of self-rule.

As Jefferson would write,

"All legitimate authority is derived from the consent of the governed.

Harry Jaffa, a constitutional expert at Claremont Institute, noted:

"Sovereignty, then, has its ground in the natural right to rule oneself that every human being possesses. Sovereignty in the political sense—what we ordinarily call sovereignty—arises when men transfer their right to rule themselves to a civil society, which can do for them what they cannot do for themselves. Natural equality leads to the social contract which leads to majority rule. But majority rule is the means to implement the equal rights of all: all who have consented to be fellow citizens, and therefore have consented to majority rule."

In other words, Jefferson's use of the term "consent" is connected to political sovereignty, natural rights, equality, and self-government, all of which are based upon the social obligation of the parties to the constitutional contract to reciprocate in obeying the rule of law, when citizens leave the state of nature.

In contrast to political sovereignty, economic sovereignty resides in the market exchange economy that provides all citizens with an equal opportunity to obtain financial success.

The political and economic sovereignty of the nation was eliminated in the transition from a sovereign geographical nation to the one-world government of the New World Order because Madison's defective constitution did not identify either citizen self rule or economic sovereignty as the mission of the nation.

Sovereignty in the United States now resides in the sovereign power of large corporations to direct the benefits of global trade to themselves, independent of the will of the citizens.

Under modern corporate globalism, we argue that the income and wealth benefits of global economic growth are internalized and captured by large corporations in their global corporate vertical value chains.

In the modern version of U. S. global corporatism, the large corporations are the dominant political partners, and the United States government is the subordinate partner, who does the bidding of the senior partner corporations.

To paraphrase Madison in Federalist #10, the representative assembly, still exists as a faux republic, constituted by a self-selected chosen body of citizens, who refine and enlarge the definition of the public purpose and whose wisdom may best discern the "true interests of the country."

In other words, the true interests of the nation reside in the true interests of the corporations to manage the global economy, for their own benefit.

The force that replaced Madison's divine right of the natural aristocracy to rule over common citizens has been replaced by the divine right of large corporations to rule in a one-world government, whose rules they create, in their rules-based global order.

In his article titled, "America's Ruling Class — And the Perils of Revolution," Angelo M. Codevilla explains how the new ruling class elites operate outside the rule of law.

Codevilla used the example of how the elites used tax money to bail themselves out of the global financial crisis, in the Fall of 2008.

Codevilla wrote,

"The leaders of the Republican and Democratic parties, agreed that spending $700 billion to buy the investors' "toxic assets" was the only alternative to the U.S. economy's "systemic collapse." In this, President George W. Bush and his would-be Republican successor John McCain agreed with the Democratic candidate, Barack Obama."

The decisions by the political elites, in 2008, were reached in secret with global corporations and central bankers.

The decisions primarily benefited three large investment banks, who are the main movers and shakers of the unelected, unaccountable, deep state agents in the capital.

In their research effort aimed at quantifying the effect of crony capitalism on national economic growth rates, Russell Sobel and Rachel Graefe-Anderson examined what type of firms gained the greatest benefit from political activities, after the 2008 bailouts. (The Relationship between Political Connections and the Financial Performance of Industries & Firms, Mercatus Working Paper, SSRN, 2018.).

They write,

"The terms "crony capitalism" and "cronyism" are now widely used to describe the modern relationship between government and private business. Cronyism is a system in which success in business is determined by political connections rather than [competitive] market forces... In this paper we empirically measure the extent to which both industry-level and firm level performance is determined by political connections rather than the normal forces of the marketplace. Our measure of "cronyism" is based on lobbying expenditures, campaign expenditures, or a combination of the two. We specifically focus on lobbying expenditures for a large part of our analysis because, as discussed below, such [rent seeking] expenditures have increased dramatically over our time frame."

What they concluded was that the main beneficiaries of crony capitalism were the senior executives at each global corporation.

They write,

"Thus, our main finding suggests that the top executives of firms are the ones who are able to capture the benefits of firm political connections across firms in the United States.

In only the case of the banking and finance industries do we see any evidence that measures of firm financial performance are positively influenced by political activities robust at both the industry and firm levels...Even if [the financial performance] of corporations benefit from political spending, those benefits may go primarily to management rather than to shareholders. This would be especially troubling because it could indicate market distortion as well as agency costs within a subset of firms."

In other words, corporate cronyism benefits members of the American ruling class, in the internal social networks of the corrupt New World Order.

Stated another way, global corporate cronyism does not benefit American middle class and working class citizens. It benefits the political, banking and corporate ruling class elites.

They cite the relationship between the largest corporate political contributions and the corporations who obtained the highest payouts from the government bailouts, after the economic collapse of 2008.

Company	Government TARP/ARRA Bailout
American International Group (AIG)	$40 billion
Citigroup	$45 billion+$306 billion in asset guarantees
BankofAmerica	$45billion+$1.1 trillion in asset guarantees
JPMorgan Chase	$25 billion
Wells Fargo	$25 billion
GMAC Financial Services	$27.3 billion
Goldman Sachs	$10 billion
Morgan Stanley	$10 billion

Sources: Bauer (2010), Kiel (2008), Recovery.gov (2012).

Both political parties, for different reasons, promote globalization of the American economy, to the detriment of the sovereign national economic interest.

The transition to global crony corporatism began during World War II, which placed the U. S. economy on a permanent war footing, after the War ended.

According to Todd Zywicki,

"During the Second World War, changes to defense contracting created the foundations for peak cronyism (see Higgs 2012: 214-218). Procurement laws were changed to allow for the widespread use of non-compete, cost-plus-fixed fee contracts, as compared to sealed competitive bids. The purpose of this change was to incentivize businesses to enter the military sector (Higgs 2006: 36-40). This led to a change in the relationship between government and private business…post-World War II period with the creation of a "permanent war economy" to engage in constant preparation and production for future wars (see Duncan and Coyne 2013a,b). The permanent war economy, which continues to thrive today, is the epitome of crony capitalism." (Zywicki, Todd J. Rent-Seeking, Crony Capitalism, and the Crony Constitution, George Mason Legal Studies Research Paper No. LS 15-08; George Mason Law & Economics Research Paper No. 15-26. August 26, 2015. Available at SSRN).

Zywicki notes that,

"The U.S. Department of Defense is the country's largest employer with 1.4 million men and women on active duty, 850,000 civilian employees, 836,000 Select Reserves and 245,000 Individual Ready Reserve forces (Department of Defense 2015: 6). These numbers do not include the significant number of people who work in jobs that supply the U.S. military with various goods and services which is estimated to total over 1.5 million (Reich 2010). Beyond the labor market, the U.S. military also influences a wide range of industries (Coyne and Hall 2018). A review of the top 100 defense contractors for FY 2016 finds recipients from the following industries: aerospace, computer and technology, accounting and professional services, courier services, engineering and construction, finance and private equity, health care, higher education, and telecommunications."

Michael Munger and Mario Villarreal-Diaz point out that,

"Decisions [about defense spending] are not made based on the "national interest" or to provide for the "common defense" of the nation. Instead, the foundation and operation of the industry is based on political relationships, favors, and privilege."

They write,

"Thus, nobody [elected representatives at the federal level] has a strong vested interest in promoting and defending free markets…every industry or occupation that has enough political power to utilize the state [federal government] will seek to control entry [of new firms]. In addition, the regulatory policy will often be so fashioned as to retard the rate of growth of new firms." (The Road to Crony Capitalism, The Independent Review, Winter 2019.).

The global crony corporate political system evolved from this permanent U. S. government war footing.

Zywicki writes,

"In order to secure contracts from the U.S. government, private firms must participate in, and successfully navigate, the political and bureaucratic process that defines the sector. Both firms and political actors attempt to influence and manipulate this process in pursuit of their own interests. The cumulative result is an entanglement of private firms with the federal government resulting in the well-known "military-industrial-congressional complex" (see Higgs 2012: 204-224, Duncan and Coyne 2013a,b, Coyne, Michaluk, and Reese 2016).

We argue that the cumulative result of global crony capitalism is the independent will of the government that is independent of the will of the consent of the governed.

We argue that rent-seeking, and its opposite, rent extraction, has replaced vote-seeking in the new American political order.

Zywicki writes that,

"Rent seeking expenditures are best understood as legal bribes whereby donors [corporations] seek to establish or maintain favorable terms with political actors [elected represenatives] in exchange for future benefits. As Higgs (2012: 214) notes, "[b]oth the givers and receivers understand these payments in exactly the same way that they understand illegal forms of bribery, even though they never admit this understanding in public."

These destructive economic and political trends could not have occurred without the political support of government agents and elected representatives to promote an agenda of globalization of trade across formerly permanent national boundaries.

In other words, they could not have occurred if Madison's constitution had clearly defined the constitutional public purpose of national economic sovereignty.

We agree with Munger that no elected representative in Washington has a vested interest in promoting free markets because Madison left that goal out of the Constitution.

In exchange for their political support for globalization policies, government agents and elected representatives extract rents from the corporations in order to obtain a share of the increased corporate profits gained by U. S. corporations in global trade.

The essence of the political bargain, after 1992, for elected U. S. representatives was placing the improvement of their own financial welfare ahead of an imaginary constitutional public purpose of improving the welfare of working class and middle class American citizen

In their economic research on the negative economic effects of corporate corruption on national economic growth, Munger and Villarreal-Diaz cite the political control that corporations have over the pace and direction of technology innovation.

They write,

"It [crony capitalism] is a social system where the government intervenes aggressively into the economy, typically with political instruments that benefit large corporations and enterprises to the detriment of smaller businesses and private citizens. Such instruments include subsidies, tariffs, import quotas, exclusive production privileges such as licenses, antitrust laws, and compulsory cartelization designs…"Innovators [entrepreneurs] are blocked from introducing new products or processes We would argue that successful [crony] capitalism leads to an impulse on the part of economic powers [global corporations] and political agents to restrict and control the destructive power of entrepreneurship. This unholy partnership [between national governments and large corporations] is "rational" in the sense that the participants [politicians and corporate executives] benefit, in some cases creating wealth and privilege [for corporations] far beyond any other mechanism that is available to them."

In their article, "The Relationship between Political Connections and the Financial Performance of Industries & Firms," Russell Sobel and Rachel Graefe-Anderson examined the effect of cronyism on the economic performance of firms. (Mercatus Working Paper, SSRN. 2018.).

They write,

"These [corporate political] donations are made largely through PAC contributions, rising from $287 million during the 2006 election cycle to $503 million during the 2008 election cycle and $319 million during the 2010 election cycle. Some of the industrial sectors to which ARRA money [bailout funds] is specifically targeted, such as energy, have seen the biggest increases in lobbying activity, with a 66 percent increase in federal lobbying expenditures between 2007 and 2010. The industry now spends over $450 million annually on lobbying and is represented by over 2,200 registered federal lobbyists. Similarly, the energy sector has increased its donations to federal political campaigns, raising them from $51 million during the 2006 election cycle to $81 million during the 2008 election cycle, and $76 million during the 2010 election cycle."

Our term for this corruption between elected representatives and corporate lobbyists is "global crony corporate capitalism," which is one variety of capitalism in the world today.

Zywicki explains,

"In the United States, the term "crony capitalism" refers to a political/economic system that resembles traditional political "corporatism." As used here, it describes a system in which government, big business, and powerful interest groups (especially labor unions) work together to further their joint interests. Government protects and subsidizes powerful corporations and in (implicit) exchange the government uses those businesses to carry out government policies outside of the ordinary processes of government."

We contrast global crony corporate capitalism with new venture creation entrepreneurial capitalism, which we argue, in the next chapter, is the only solution for middle class citizens out of the economic destruction of the New World Order. (Vass, Laurie Thomas, The American Millennial Attraction to Socialism: Comparing the Economies of Chinese Communism, Crony Corporate Capitalism, European Crony Socialism, and the American Free Enterprise Innovation Economy, Gabby Press, 2020.).

Christopher J. Coyne and Abigail R Hall write,

"Under crony capitalism politicians and regulators use businesses to advance the interests of politicians and interest groups in a symbiotic relationship: government creates rents [tax spending] and then distributes them to itself and favored interests. Many of the relationships that grew up during the [2008] financial crisis and its aftermath through legislation such as the Dodd-Frank financial reform legislation illustrate the differences between crony capitalism and mere rent-seeking. (Cronyism: Necessary for the Minimal, Protective State, GMU Working Paper in Economics No. 18-26 SSRN. July 2018.).

Zywicki places U. S. corporate cronyism into an economic exchange framework to demonstrate that that the parties who benefit from the crony exchange exploit those who bear the costs of cronyism. [middle and working class citizens].

Zywicki states,

"In the (implicit crony) exchange, the firm promises to share some of that surplus with politically-favored groups, such as labor unions or favored interest groups (such as environmental groups), and with the politicians themselves through campaign contributions and other means of support. Thus, the firms and their managers and shareholders gain what amounts to a sinecure and protection from the gales of creative destruction, and, in exchange, politicians can divert some of this flow of resources to their preferred policies and groups." (Rent-Seeking, Crony Capitalism, and the Crony Constitution, SSRN. 2015.).

Three different economic forces combined in the 4 decades from 1980 to 2020 to exacerbate the transition away from nominal national economic sovereignty to a globalist crony capitalist economy.

First, beginning around 1980, many of the repetitive tasks in U. S. manufacturing jobs were replaced by computer integrated manufacturing.

Second, beginning around 1992, with NAFTA, and becoming more pronounced in 2001, with the entrance of China into the World Trade Organization, many U. S. manufacturing jobs were outsourced to foreign countries.

Third. the movement of manufacturing facilities to foreign countries was compounded by off-shoring intermediate manufacturing supply chains to foreign firms in India and China.

American jobs that were previously performed in the intermediate supply chains in major metro regions were eliminated, in an economic process called "hollowing out."

For every job lost in the U. S. regional intermediate technology supply chains, an additional 4 jobs were lost in the regional intermediate service sectors which supported the domestic manufacturing jobs. (Cited in Tech Starts: High-Technology Business Formation and Job Creation in the United States, Ian Hathaway, Kauffman Foundation Research Series, 2013.).

In the absence of manufacturing jobs, the displaced U. S. workers either went to work for fast food chains and motels, or they entered a permanent dependency on government welfare payments.

As a result of moving manufacturing facilities to China, the United States economy destroyed the ability of the economy to create technological innovation because the intermediate demand chains were the source of new technological knowledge.

As a result of losing the ability to create new technology, the rate of technology commercialization in U. S. new ventures dropped dramatically, from 2001 to 2020.

After 2002, when China entered the WTO, the rate of new technology firm creation had declined to the point where the U. S. economy was not generating net new jobs because the trade with China destroyed technology knowledge creation and technology knowledge diffusion in the U, S intermediate demand chains.

The immediate job loss in direct and intermediate manufacturing jobs in the U. S. economy, as a consequence of globalization, are not being replaced because all net new job growth comes from the creation of technology firms less than one year old. (Haltiwanger, John C., Jarmin, Ron S., Miranda, Javier, Who Creates Jobs? Small Vs. Large Vs. Young, NBER Working Paper 16300, 2010.).

The jobs in the seven service sectors pay much lower wages than manufacturing jobs.

As a consequence of globalism, the average U. S. worker lost 2.14% in wages during the period from 2001 to 2020.

As a consequence of global crony capitalism, when workers formerly employed in manufacturing could not find jobs, they began a life of permanent dependency on welfare payments. Welfare payments went up 2.21% per year as a result of increased imports from China. (Autor,

David H., Dorn, David, Hanson, Gordon H., The China Syndrome: Local Labor Market Effects of Import Competition In The United States, , NBER Working Paper 18054, 2012.).

Autor et al., describe that the average U. S. worker lost $492 per year, from 1990 to 2007, as a result of trade with China.

From 1980 to 2010, middle and working class occupations lost jobs. Generally, those occupations are filled by workers with a community college degree or a high school diploma.

The large increase in service sector jobs of 53%, from 1980 to 2005, documents the trend that many middle class workers who lost their jobs in manufacturing went to work in the gig labor market. (Autor, David H., and Dorn, David, The Growth of Low-Skill Service Jobs and the Polarization of the US Labor Market, American Economic Review, 2013.).

Capital investment in U. S. business declined ½% per year, from 2001 to 2020.

The average decline in U. S. economic growth is 1.48% per year, from 1990 to 2007.

The most recent iteration of corporate globalism is to replace off-shoring and outsourcing of production from the

U. S. with a new version of globalism called "Vertically Integrated Value Chains."

The social and economic impact of vertically integrated value chains on the American middle class standard of living has been devastating, even worse for middle class citizens than the direct job losses of outsourcing and off-shoring.

The Duke Center on Globalization, Governance & Competitiveness, describes the transition in globalism from many firms who are engaged in global trade to one dominant large corporation, which seeks to internalize all operations within the single legal entity.

They write,

"The activities that comprise a value chain can be contained within a single firm or divided among different firms (globalvaluechains.org, 2011). In the context of globalization, the activities that constitute a value chain have generally been carried out in inter-firm networks on a global scale. By focusing on the sequences of tangible and intangible value-adding activities, from conception and production to end use, GVC analysis provides a holistic view of global industries – both from the top-down (for example, examining how lead firms "govern" their global-scale affiliate and supplier networks) and from the bottom-up (for example, asking how these business decisions affect the trajectory of economic and social "upgrading" or "downgrading" in specific countries and regions)." (Gereffi, Gary, Fernandez-Stark, Karina, Global Value Chain Analysis: A Primer, Second Edition. The Duke Center on Globalization, Governance & Competitiveness, 2016.).

In the previous version of global corporatism, it was difficult for senior U. S. executives to manage and control the quality of goods produced in the intermediate demand chains of foreign affiliates.

Between 2002 and 2018, various attempts at Global Rules Based Governance were implemented by global corporations to overcome the quality control issues.

Rules Based Governance, in the global setting, tended to supersede contract law in different nations in favor of direct informal agreements between partners in the global value chains. (Gilson, Ronald J., et al., Contracting for Innovation: Vertical Disintegration and Interfirm Collaboration, Columbia Law and Economics Working Paper No. 340, 2009.).

As a consequence of Rules Based Governance, the sovereignty of the U. S. Constitution was also superseded and replaced by international law, administered by various international non-government agencies, such as the IMF and UN.

The vertically integrated value chains provided corporations with the market power to markup prices inside their own value chains, prior to the sale of finished goods in the global final demand markets.

In their article "Global Market Power and its Macroeconomic Implications," Diez et al., define market power,

"A standard definition of market power is the ability of a firm to maintain prices above marginal cost—the level that would prevail under perfect competition. Since data on prices and marginal costs are generally unavailable for large numbers of firms over time, much of the existing work focuses on measuring market power using sales concentration ratios at the industry level." (Díez Federico J., Leigh, Daniel and Tambunlertchai Suchanan, IMF Working Paper, WP/18/137 2018."

From 1980, at the beginning of the U. S. economic transition to a globalist economy, to 2017, U. S. firms have increase internal markups from around 18% over marginal costs to around 67% above marginal costs. (Loecker, Jan, Eeckhout, De Jan, The Rise of Market Power and The Macroeconomic Implications, NBER Working Paper 23687, 2017.).

The economic term for internal price markup power is "pure profits.," in contrast to competitive price profit.

While the rate of pure profit for 1500 large corporations has been going up, since the transition to the globalist economy, the rate of capital investment by U. S. corporations in the U. S. domestic economy has been going down.

According to Diez et al.,

"At higher levels of markups, however, increases in markups become associated with lower investment, as indicated by the negative coefficient in the second row. This finding is consistent with the "inverted-U" relation between competition and investment posited by Aghion and others (2005), where pre-innovation rents rise faster than post-innovation rents at high levels of market power, implying weaker incentives to invest.... As of 2016, higher markups are associated with lower investment for 8, 17, and 6 percent of U.S. publicly listed firms, across the three specifications, respectively. In contrast, no firms had a negative association between higher markups and investment as of 1980."

The U. S. corporations surveyed by Diez account for 79% of total U. S. GDP, in 2016.

At the same time that U. S. corporate senior executives realized the benefits of uncontrolled markups in prices to derive "pure profits," they also realized that if they could integrate all operations, from raw resource extraction to final goods delivery, that they would obtain a greater share of the wealth and income from globalism, and not be forced to share income with either workers or small firms in the intermediate demand chains in undeveloped nations.

In the previous version of globalism, intermediate demand production was performed in low wage nations, or in slave labor camps in China.

The scholars at Duke University euphemistically call that part of the low wage production as occurring in "Developing Countries," as if the citizens in those nations had some control over their location at the bottom of the global value chain.

The higher value added components of production occur at the top of the of the global value chain, which is another way of saying that "pure profits," occur in "Developed Countries."

In the recent version of globalism, the entire production chain is performed inside the legal entity of a single corporation, which allows the corporation to internalize the entire flow of income that previously would have occurred in a competitive economy comprised of many intermediate demand firms, and many production units, located in the United States.

The entire World Economic Forum propaganda argument in favor of the New World Order is that corporate globalism leads to higher rates of economic growth, for the entire world, than the economic growth rates of independent sovereign nations.

The sovereignty that counts the most in corporate globalism is world economic sovereignty in a global rules based governance framework.

The political stability of the U. S. crony capitalist version of the corporatist model depends on politically-connected special interests in western nations obtaining a flow of unearned benefits from the system, independent of any notion of sovereignty related to the U. S. Constitution.

The logic of the WEF propaganda is that the Chinese model of totalitarianism is a better economic model than free market national sovereignty. .

The flaw in the WEF New World Order economic logic is that the Chinese model is incapable of generating economic growth because it is incapable of technology innovation, unless it can steal technology from U. S. corporations.

All of the future U. S. economic growth, and all of the new job creation in the U. S. labor markets, depends on high rates of technology innovation and new product commercialization.

With the transition of the U. S. economy from domestic economic sovereignty to a global corporatist economy, the U. S. lost the ability to generate technology knowledge creation and knowledge diffusion.

We explain in our book, Updating Schumpeter's Gales of Creative Destruction,

"In the absence of real economic growth, after 2001, the U. S. economy has reverted to a permanent boom-bust-bubble economy, caused by monetary and currency manipulation, coordinated by the Fed and global central banks, not real economic growth caused by private business capital investment in new technological ventures…The mirage of economic growth of global central bank monetary manipulation, replaced the real economic growth that was formerly caused by capital investment in small technology ventures, which primarily took place in the intermediate demand networks in 300 of the largest U. S. metro regions." (Gabby Press, June 2022.).

Corporate control over the creation and diffusion of technological knowledge in the global macrotechnology is the weak link, and vulnerable point of attack, for replacing Madison's defective document with a new constitution that enshrines domestic economic sovereignty as the mission in the Preamble

Global corporations require controlled technological innovation, and global crony capitalism, in order to direct the benefits of innovation to themselves, and their crony stakeholders.

The initial factor of production that made America great was the ability of common citizens to use their ingenuity and imagination to create new ventures. That ability was based upon a common culture of the value of knowledge creation and diffusion, which caused the creation of new technology ventures.

Of all the possible causes of U. S. economic decline and the loss of U. S. economic sovereignty, the biggest single factor is loss of technological knowledge diffusion, which previously occurred in intermediate demand regional technology clusters, of very small technology firms.

Over 50% of the economic decline in the U. S. is related to a dramatic decline in the rate of technology new venture creation in the U. S. (Ufuk, Akcigit, et al., Innovation and Trade Policy in a Globalized World, NBER Working Paper 24543, 2018.).

Akcigit, et al., write that the cause of the decline in knowledge creation is linked to the power of large corporations to markup prices in the finished goods, final demand markets, as a result of their ability to vertically integrate the entire production process from start to finish.

The monopoly power of large corporations to set prices in vertically integrated global value chains depends on one crucial variable, their ability to control the pace of technological innovation, seen in the Duke research report as control over technology research.

We contrast crony corporate capitalism with new venture creation entrepreneurial capitalism, which we argue is the only solution for middle class citizens out of the economic destruction of the New World Order. (Vass, Laurie Thomas, America's Final Revolution: Reconstructing Jefferson's American Dream of An Entrepreneurial Capitalist Society. Gabby Press. 2022.).

The government, in the hands of the new corporate ruling class, has a will of its own, and that will serves the interests of large global corporations, who seek to bend the flow of income from the global value chains to themselves.

Madison's constitution is silent on how common middle class citizens can establish national economic sovereignty because his rules deliberately subordinated their interests to the interests of the natural aristocracy.

The best solution for middle class and working class citizens is to start over with a new nation and a new constitution that states that the mission of the new nation is to promote individual liberty and free market exchange.

Chapter 7. The Entrepreneurial Capitalist Constitutional Public Purpose.

The initial factor endowments of individual creativity and initiative, in 1776, created an unassailable American global comparative advantage in technological innovation and new venture creation.

In the context of a new constitutional preamble, promoting this initial American factor endowment as the constitutional purpose would be called creating a "commonwealth of independent producers." (Vass, Laurie Thomas, Equal Rights For All. Special Privileges for None. Re-Examining the Agrarian Arguments Against A Centralized American Government, Gabby Press. 2017.).

In contrast to Madison's Preamble of forming a "more perfect union," that was modeled upon the British two social class conflict model, a better alternative would have been modeled upon the Locke-Mason-Jefferson philosophical value of individual liberty.

Our main economic argument in favor of using the Locke-Mason-Jefferson version of the American constitution, in 1776, is that it would have led to the emergence of a stable middle class social order, which would have eliminated the ruling class' justification, in 1787, to seek unearned advantage [shared plunder] through unelected ruling class power to manipulate money supply and interest rates. (Vass, Laurie Thomas, George Mason's America: The State Sovereignty Alternative to Madison's Centralized American Ruling Class Aristocracy, Gabby Press. 2023.).

Our argument, today, for replacing Madison's flawed constitution is that his arrangement of power, initially reserved for the benefit of the natural aristocracy, has been captured by a new, and even more tyrannical power, that we call global crony corporate capitalism.

The Locke-Mason-Jefferson philosophical lineage of liberty creates the conditions of free market capitalism because it is based upon the idea that individuals are their own best judge of improving their welfare, through free market exchange.

The primary constitutional economic goal is a high annual rate of private capital investment in technology and new small entrepreneurial firms, decentralized to the major metropolitan regions of the states.

The maintenance and preservation of a stable middle class social order depends on high rates of economic growth, whose income benefits are distributed widely through the direct and indirect value chains in a sovereign national economy.

We argue that the social welfare outcomes of entrepreneurial capitalism are more "fair" than either the outcomes of the Democrat Marxist economic hoax or Madison's shared plunder natural aristocracy of elite rule.

The same principle of individual liberty in economic free market exchange forms the basis of Jefferson's political principles of self-government, based upon equal natural rights.

Jefferson offered a revolutionary theory of government, based upon equal rights, which created the conditions of entrepreneurial capitalism, which Jefferson, in that colonial time period, called the community of small independent farmers.

Today, Jefferson's faith in the agrarian farmer economy would be called entrepreneurial capitalism, where citizens have an equal opportunity to achieve happiness and prosperity through individual initiative. (Vass, Laurie Thomas, America's Final Revolution: Reconstructing Jefferson's American Dream of An Entrepreneurial Capitalist Society, Gabby Press. 2022.).

We argue that there is only one economic system that attempts to maximize individual welfare, which we call the Entrepreneurial Capitalist Economy.

Further, following the constitutional creation process of James Buchanan, we argue that there is only one constitutional configuration of rules that creates the Entrepreneurial Capitalist Constitutional Public Purpose.

That single constitutional configuration creates the maximum level of trust among citizens, so that citizens can trust each other to obey the rule of law in economic exchanges, especially when reciprocity in trust occurs in the future time period.

In the individualist entrepreneurial capitalist society, fairness constitutes the ability of the individual to appropriate the income that they produce through free market exchange.

We believe that it was this concept of Jefferson's entrepreneurial capitalist society, which the 13 states were attempting to create in 1776, when they left the state of nature to form their first constitutional contract, called the Articles of Confederation.

We also believe that it was this individualist, entrepreneurial society that Madison correctly perceived to be a threat to the ruling class privileges of the American natural aristocracy, if the common citizens in America ever formed a unified middle class ideology of liberty.

Coincidentally, that same constitutional configuration of trust and fair exchange, also creates the institutional environment for maximum rates of technological knowledge creation and knowledge diffusion among citizens.

Maximum rates of knowledge creation create the social conditions for maximum rates of technology innovation, which creates maximum rates of economic growth.

We conclude that the progress towards a fair American entrepreneurial economy can be visualized as a knowledge creation enterprise, modeled upon the logic of a regional metro block chain, whose end goal is the commercialization of radical new technology, and the creation of new future markets.

The mission of the nation, or constitutional public purpose, of the government economic policy is to increase private domestic capital investment, which then:

- Creates new interindustry supply chains in each metro regional economy,
- Diffuses innovation and knowledge among supply chain member firms,
- Creates high rates of entrepreneurial new venture creation in technology industrial clusters,
- Creates new future markets that distribute income and creates jobs with internal career paths,
- Creates the capital market dynamic of capital reinvestment of profits from one time period into the future time periods, via new regional capital market institutions.

In the period of time, after the citizens leave the state of nature, and have agreed upon social rules of cooperation, the new constitutional rules of representation would allow for the development of the institutional market framework of economic exchange, including the institutional configuration of the banking and monetary system.

In both Hobbes, and Locke, when citizens leave the state of nature, to form civil society, they arrive in the new civil society with certain attributes and resources that they took with them from the state of nature.

In both concepts of the rule of law, one attribute that all citizens possessed when they leave the state of nature was their property of self.

Locke, (1694), disagreed with Hobbes, (1648), about the force that compelled citizen obedience to the "natural rights" rule of law.

Locke called this human attribute of self, labor property, to distinguish it from land property.

As Locke noted,

"Now of those good things which Nature hath provided in common, every one had a Right...to as much as he could use, and had a Property in all that he could affect with his Labour: all that his Industry could extend to, to alter from the State of Nature had put it in, was his. He that gathered a Hundred Bushels of acorns or apples, had thereby a Property in them; they were his Goods as soon as he gathered."

When the citizens leave the state of nature, the fundamental justification of government, according to Locke, is to protect those natural rights with the rule of law.

After the new constitution is ratified, citizens agree to obey the rule of law, in Locke, because they share the cultural value of personal gain from using their own labor private property to create economic value, for themselves.

For Locke, value is defined as "use value," or the internal happiness created by using the private labor property.

For Locke, the market exchange price of a commodity was based upon its usefulness and its scarcity, not just on the amount of labor that was used, (Marx, 1867), as a factor of production, to produce the good.

The greatest economic value is created, in Locke, when individuals have the greatest liberty to create whatever products that causes happiness for themselves.

In the Second Treatise on Government, Locke argued that all people had an equal right to mix their labor with common, unowned, resources to create private property, both in consumable goods and from farming the land.

The right to own private property was unlimited and use value in the sale of the goods was determined from the eyes of the parties to the exchange.

Karen Vaughn, in "John Locke and the Labor Theory of Value," makes this important distinction between market exchange value, based upon prices, versus moral exchange value, based upon Locke's concept of the natural rights rule of law. (Journal of Libertarian Studies, Volume 2, Number 4.1978.).

Vaughn writes,

"Natural law dictated that all men had common access to God's earthly resources, and that each man had a natural right to self ownership which, when coupled with his right and duty to survive, permitted him to create private property where none previously existed."

Vaughn concludes her analysis of Locke by noting that his thoughts about government were the foundation of the original American system of the rule of law, codified in the Articles of Confederation.

"The concept of self ownership is not only a cornerstone of individualism and personal freedom, but is also an invitation to social and economic mobility. (The American) commercial economy thrives on the transfer of resources to those who can make them most profitable. It was just this kind of resource mobility that Locke's Labor theory of property and his theory of market value justified, in his system. One earned property through one's own efforts, but the (use) value of that property was determined by the market."

The way that Vaughn says this is that private property in Locke is,

"an invitation to social and economic mobility."

Over time, this attribute of Locke's economic system became known, in America, as the shared aspiration of upward occupational and social mobility. The common phrase for this value was "self-made man."

For Locke, private property in the market exchange system benefits everyone because the use of labor property adds economic value to all products, that are subsequently available for exchange. (Smith, 1776.).

Locke's use of the term "natural rights," and his invocation of God, defines labor property in a moral sense, not simply in a price-based market exchange sense. The "value" created by mixing labor with nature's resources, including unoccupied land, possesses the attribute of a moral natural right.

Mason and Jefferson modified Locke's natural right of property by adding a natural right of equal liberty to use their labor to create prosperity.

In Mason's treatment of the private labor property, Mason added to Locke's treatment the right of citizens to obtain future prosperity, through market exchange.

In his 1775 address to the assembled militia in Fairfax County, Virginia, Mason said,

"We came equals into this world, and equals shall we go out of it. All men are by nature born equally free and independent. To protect the weaker from the injuries and insults of the stronger were societies first formed; when men entered into compacts to give up some of their natural rights, that by union and mutual assistance they might secure the rest; but they gave up no more than the nature of the thing required. Every society, all government, and every kind of civil impact therefore, is or ought to be, calculated for the general good and safety of the community. Every power, every authority vested in particular men is, or ought to be, ultimately directed to this sole end; and whenever any power or authority whatever extends further, or is of longer duration than is in its nature necessary for these purposes, it may be called government, but it is in fact oppression."

In his book about Mason, Robert Rutland cites John Locke as the source of Mason's individualist philosophy.

Rutland writes,

[Mason believed] "that men are entitled to the means of acquiring and possessing property marked an historic advance from John Locke's trilogy of rights—life, liberty, and property—that simply endorsed ownership of property…Contained within it was an unlimited faith in free men to make the proper decision under any circumstances. A government is the creation of the people, who can maintain or abolish it—whichever they choose. This was not philosophical speculation, an hypothesis for quiet, fireside analysis. It was a course of action." (Rutland, Robert A., George Mason: Reluctant Statesman, 1961.).

Rutland makes the important point that Mason extended Locke's proviso on unlimited property in the state of nature, to the additional principle, in Mason, that citizens have a right to both acquire, and a right to use property, to advance their own prosperity.

In Jefferson's treatment of the natural rights of labor property, the phrase,

"endowed by their Creator with certain unalienable Rights, that among these are Life, Liberty and the pursuit of Happiness," he is using Locke's definition of happiness as use value.

In the Declaration, it is the shared cultural values of life, liberty and happiness that bind citizens together into a unified culture, and the natural rights that the new Nation sought to protect.

The relationship between constitutional individual freedom and national economic growth is through the ability of individuals to create new technology ventures that commercialize new technology products.

The new technology products create new future markets that create new flows of income.

Technical change causes new income flows to be created where none had existed before. Part of the new income is a result of increased productivity, meaning that output increases with reduced inputs in the production unit.

Part of the new income is in the form of profits related to new goods produced by new production units.

Another part of the income is in the form of wages and salaries paid to people who work in the new units, who spend their incomes in the local economy, creating income and employment multipliers.

The single, unique configuration of rules that produce maximum social welfare economic outcomes, according to James Buchanan, were fair rules of exchange, based upon maximum individual freedom.

The rules of the individualist constitution must be fair and aim at achieving a specific set of goals:

- Allowing individuals to obtain fair reward for work.
- Providing incentives to work.
- Providing an equal path to individual prosperity.

Voluntary cooperation to obey the rule of law between individuals occurs when the individuals assume, prior to entering into any political or financial exchange process, that other citizens share these common cultural and political values.

In The Reason of Rules, Buchanan and Brennan write,

"Our specific claim is that justice takes its meaning from the rules for the social order within which notions of justice are to be applied. To appeal to considerations of justice is to appeal to relevant rules. These rules provide the framework within which patterns of distributional end states emerge from the interaction of persons who play various complex functional roles." (The Reason of Rules: Constitutional Political Economy, 2000.).

Fair and just rules are created by rational individuals, with a rationality based upon self preservation and gaining future prosperity.

Buchanan relies upon the rationality of individual self-interest as a force that binds individuals to obey the rule of law, through a mental process of rationally minimizing risk in uncertain decision making environments.

In leaving the state of nature, and forming a constitution, Buchanan explains, individuals are placed in a position of uncertainty in the outcome of their life's mission.

No individual knows in advance where the individual may end up, given the choice between one set of constitutional rules or another.

In the absence of certainty about the rules of society, individuals tend to abandon cultural values of trust, truth and honesty in favor of self-oriented values. (shared plunder.).

As Buchanan points out, voluntary allegiance to the rule of law results from the realization that it is in one's rational best interest for his or her life's mission to be consistent with the public purpose of the constitutional rule of law.

Common cultural values depend further upon a set of social and political institutions that act as the medium through which the future obligations are discharged.

Cultural values, in other words, provide an essential set of conditions for pro-social rule adherence in political exchanges involving trust.

One of our main arguments for civil dissolution and national divorce is that the American society no longer adheres to a common set of cultural and moral values.

The ideological conflict between natural rights conservatives and Democrat Marxists is irreconcilable under Madison's constitution.

Buchanan argued that the only unambiguous goal of the constitutional public purpose is economic growth. (Buchanan, James M. The Logical Foundations of Constitutional Liberty, Liberty Fund. 1999.).

The only fair and logical way to measure growth and improvements in social welfare is to add up, or aggregate, individual welfare into a macro economic measure of national income.

Buchanan argued that the state, as a collectivist agency, did not have an omnipotent, all knowing "fiscal brain," that seeks to maximize social welfare. (Buchanan, James M., "Rent Seeking and Profit Seeking," in, James M. Buchanan, Robert Tollison, and Gordon Tullock (eds). Toward a Theory of the Rent-Seeking Society. 1980.).

This placed Buchanan in philosophical opposition to both Madison's concept that the natural aristocracy knew what was best for common citizens better than the individuals themselves, and in ideological opposition to modern day Democrat Marxists, who claim that central economic planning yields better social welfare outcomes than free market exchange outcomes.

Both of those competing ideologies are based upon a synthetic, imaginary social welfare function that elites profess to maximize.

Buchanan argued that there is no grand social welfare function that virtuous elected representatives attempt to maximize. The welfare that politicians maximize is their own financial welfare, through the crony system of shared plunder.

The economic and political decisions by federal elected representatives are not made based upon the "national interest" or to provide for the "common defense" of the nation.

Instead, the foundation and operation of the national economy, through the operations of the Federal Reserve Bank, and foreign policy decisions, are based upon crony capitalism in the military-industrial corrupt political relationships, aimed at maintaining the privileges of American ruling class elites.

In The Reason of Rules, (2000), Buchanan and Brennan explain the importance of how citizens create fair constitutional rules, based upon an original consent of the citizens to obey the rules that they give to themselves.

Consent is provided in the initial agreement of creating the constitution, and then, afterwards, in a process of on-going consent.

Buchanan addressed this question of fairness in his book, The Theory of Public Choice, (1984), in terms of on-going citizen consent, after citizens give the initial grant of consent to abide by the rules.

After the citizens give their prior consent to the initial creation of the rules, as they did in 1781, with the ratification of the Articles of Confederation, fair rules would have allowed them to give ongoing consent, after the government had been established.

Common citizens were not provided this fair opportunity to consent to Madison's unfair rules, either in the original consent, or in the defective rules of citizen representation in Madison's extended republic.

In the context of the application of fair constitutional rules, Buchanan makes a distinction between justice in political rules and justice in economic exchanges.

Both economic and political justice are based upon the concept of the equal application of the rule of law to all citizens, or more commonly, equality before the law.

However, after the constitution has been created, Buchanan's method of justice entails the creation of social and economic institutions that adjudicate the law.

One for political rights, and one for economic justice.

If the institutions are designed to adjudicate rights, then the rule of law can be applied uniformly.

If, on the other hand, Madison's institutions were conceived in the initial constitution as the mechanism to separate and balance political powers, then rights adjudication becomes more uncertain, contributing to the social uncertainty about rule adherence.

The political/judicial institutions act as the equivalent of the price-based market mechanism that coordinates voluntary behavior in free market transactions.

In order to perform the function of coordinating mutually beneficial joint behavior that has as its consequence pro-social rules adherence, both institutions must reflect the underlying cultural values of trust and truth, which must be universally held by all individuals who are parties to the original constitutional contract.

"Just conduct," writes Buchanan, "consists of behavior that does not violate rules to which one has given prior consent."

We argue that one of Madison's moral flaws is that common citizens, in the 13 states, were never granted the opportunity to provide prior consent to be ruled by Madison's natural aristocracy.

Buchanan applies this concept of the limited power of institutions to his suggestions about the relationship between free markets and governmental power.

He states that,

"...for most persons, the independence offered by the presence of market alternatives offers the maximal liberty possible. But we have not yet designed institutions that will satisfy the individual's search for community in the impersonal setting of the market order without, at the same time, undermining the very independence that this order affords."

The point he makes is that certain types of institutional arrangements, for example the Federal Reserve Bank, damage individual freedom gained in free market economic exchange.

Buchanan's rules link individual choice, in the free market system, to individual choice in the political system, because economic individualism is linked to equal political natural rights.

No other constitutional configuration starts out with this set of equal natural rights, aiming at the social goal to create "maximum" individual happiness.

No other constitutional configuration starts out with the initial assumption that individual happiness, in politics, is linked to individual liberty, in economics.

There is nothing preordained or certain in the outcome of technical innovation that would automatically create more future wealth or greater income.

Schumpeter explained that there are social, political, and economic forces that favor one type of technical change, and there are other political forces that favor status quo technical change.

National economic growth is a contingent outcome of the type of technical change, in the economy. It occurs in some nations, but not in others.

In The Lever of Riches: Technological Creativity and Economic Progress, (1990), Joel Mokyr reviews the relationship between economic development and technological innovation by first raising the question why economic growth occurs in some societies and not in others.

According to Mokyr, economic growth results from open flows of knowledge, which only occur under one configuration of constitutional rules advocated by Buchanan.

According to Mokyr, technological progress tends to occur in national economies which have well-educated citizens, who are deeply engaged in the economic and political decisions of their communities.

In such a society, the appearance of new technical knowledge is rapidly diffused, and as the knowledge embodied in the change spreads among citizens, it creates imbalances and bottlenecks in existing interindustry relations.

These imbalances are important as an explanation of economic growth caused by technical change because they create the conditions for new, future, interindustry relationships as the imbalances and bottlenecks are overcome.

The new interindustry relationships tend to create new sources of income that are not dependent on the older interindustry relationships.

Mokyr found in his historical review that certain political organizations and social groups are opposed to open knowledge flows because that type of technical change would tend to disrupt the advantages they receive from the existing status quo arrangement of power.

In the modern setting, we have called this arrangement of power global crony capitalism, as visualized in the new vertically integrated value chains.

Clayton Christensen suggests that there are two types of technological innovation, each one with a different macro economic outcome. (The Innovator's Dilemma: The Revolutionary Book That Will Change the Way You Do Business. 2011.).

The two types of innovation have been described as "disruptive technology innovation," and "sustaining innovation."

Following Mokyr, in the new global crony capitalist setting, the large corporation seek to inhibit knowledge creation and diffusion in order to direct the benefits of technical change to themselves, in their vertically integrated value chains.

All of Christensen's descriptions are based on how large multinational corporations manage the issue of technological innovation, within the administrative institutional entity of a corporation.

In The Innovator's Dilemma, Christensen suggests that radical new products cut into the low end of the current marketplace and eventually evolve to the point where the new products displace high-end competitors and their reigning technologies.

When global companies are blind-sided by the new competition, Christensen calls this phenomenon "disruptive technology." (Polaroid cameras disrupted by the cell phone, yellow book telephone pages disrupted by Amazon).

In contrast to disruptive innovation, Christensen describes "sustaining innovation" as improvements to existing products, to make them more user friendly.

Radical technology innovation is the cause of economic growth because radical innovation creates new future markets. Sustaining technology innovation does not cause the creation of new future markets, and does not cause economic growth.

Radical technical change is produced by open flows of knowledge.

The other type of technical change diffuses technical knowledge in closed, proprietary flows of knowledge.

Economic growth caused by technical change is a result of capital investments made by entrepreneurs in new production units that create new interindustry relationships and new market relationships that did not exist before.

The new ventures produce products whose supply varies, according to the feedback mechanism of consumer preferences.

From a macro economic perspective, sustaining innovations do not create new future markets, and without the creation of new future markets there is no economic growth.

New markets caused by radical technology innovation tends to destroy the status quo distributions of income, wealth, and political power in the current global corporate capitalist system. (Vass, Laurie Thomas, Predicting Technology, Gabby Press, 2007.).

The macro economic results of radical technological innovation are often totally unforeseen and unanticipated, and involve the emergence of entirely new final demand markets and brand new intermediate demand value chains.

In other words, in the open knowledge creation society, those values of individual liberty function to allow citizens to obtain financial benefits in the future from investments or loans that they make today.

When those political values are shared and wide-spread, citizens in the natural rights republic obey the rule of law.

Obedience and allegiance to the rule of law occurs as a result of economic growth defined as the constitutional public purpose.

William Baumol explained that the economic growth in the United States, during the 1990's was due to high rates of new venture creation in high technology sectors.

Baumol, (et al.) wrote,

"Productivity growth and innovation in the United States in the 1990s, was made possible largely by new, innovative companies, and not by the established giants that had previously dominated the U.S. economic landscape. Something new was afoot, and to one of us, it was sufficiently important to merit a special label: "entrepreneurial capitalism," (Baumol, William J., Litan, Robert E., and Schramm, Carl J., Good Capitalism, Bad Capitalism, and the Economics of Growth and Prosperity, 2007.).

In contrast to global corporate crony capitalism, Baumol cites Joseph Schumpeter's term, "entrepreneurial capitalism," as the cause of economic growth and prosperity.

Baumol also cites Paul Romer on the causes of economic growth.

Baumol notes,

"Romer went one step further, observing that technological advances often were not simply by-products, but were the objects of economic activity itself—the products of deliberate investments of time and money by individuals and firms seeking to improve on what already exists and ultimately to commercialize any successful results. In this sense, business firms' investment in knowledge creation is analogous to their investment in new equipment that promises to make employees more productive. But unlike investment in a new machine, which has more or less predictable productivity-enhancing consequences, investment in knowledge discovery (and, if successful, its subsequent commercialization) is fraught with uncertainty. (Romer, Paul, What Drives Economic Growth, 2018.).

Economic growth in entrepreneurial capitalism occurs as a result of an entrepreneur taking old knowledge, gained from using the old technology, in the old unit, with her when she leaves with her new technological knowledge, to create the new venture.

The new ventures are more productive, and achieve higher overall production output per unit of input than the old production units.

To the extent that a metro region has a high rate, or pace of technical learning, and has accumulated technical knowledge, it will have a high rate of technical change in production processes, and consequently, a high rate of economic growth, as a result of entrepreneurs creating new ventures.

However, innovating firms, and the presence of social-business networks, and the accumulation of technological knowledge, are not distributed uniformly across regions.

In addition, entrepreneurial capitalism threatens the status quo arrangement of political power in the global crony capitalist economy.

Piero Saviotti notes that innovative firms,

"...tend to cluster in those (areas) that were already innovating countries...this specificity cannot be explained by factor endowments, but is more likely to be caused by specific institutional configurations, and by the cumulative, local and specific character of the knowledge that the institutions possess." (Saviotti, Piero, Technological Evolution, Variety and the Economy, 1996.).

This tendency of firms to concentrate in a geographic region contributes to the development of a regional economic "macrotechnology."

According to Saviotti, the reason one metro region economy develops a macrotechnology, as opposed to any other region is related to the,

"...specific institutional configurations and by the cumulative, local, and specific character of the knowledge that the institutions possess."

The geographically-specific technological knowledge in a metro region facilitates the ability of all the firms to absorb new technological knowledge, which we argue is enhanced by the blockchain technology, which we describe in Updating Schumpeter's Gales of Creative Destruction: Exploiting the Vulnerability of New World Order Corporate Globalism With Regional Blockchain Entrepreneurial Economic Growth, (Gabby Press. 2022.).

Richard Florida, in "The Distinct Personality of Entrepreneurial Cities," (2015), explains the connection between the entrepreneurial culture and tacit knowledge creation.

Florida states,

"The entrepreneurial culture (an environment that fosters entrepreneurship) creates an economy where entrepreneurs have the drive and resilience to overcome obstacles, are more open to new ideas, and are able to connect with people, build and lead teams, and get things done... The entrepreneurial culture interacts with and connects to local (tacit) knowledge and talent. As Renfrow puts it, "new knowledge will have a greater propensity to generate entrepreneurship in regions with a pronounced entrepreneurial culture where the predominant attitudes and norms reinforce an individual's decisions to act upon entrepreneurial opportunities." (Bloomberg, 2015.).

The entire economic growth strategy of entrepreneurial capitalism is based upon creating a constitution that allows individual citizens to seek wealth and prosperity.

The function of government at the national, state and regional metro level consists of implementing institutions that facilitate economic growth through technology commercialization in new venture creation.

We agree with the advice of Baumol that the implementation of the entrepreneurial capitalist growth model in the new constitution, requires elected representatives to adopt a new perspective on how they view their region.

Baumol writes,

[Elected representatives need to see their] economies as potential "growth machines," which need fuel to operate but which also must have some essential primary parts or components that work in harmony if they are to promote entrepreneurship, innovation (and its dissemination), and growth most effectively. The "fuel" for an economy is the right set of macroeconomic policies: essentially, prudent fiscal and monetary policies to keep inflation low and relatively stable and to prevent economic downturns (or even worse, financial crises) from derailing progress toward growth in the long run…The key is not so much how incomes are currently distributed [via rent seeking] but rather the ease or difficulty that individuals have of climbing to higher economic stations and thus to earning higher incomes. In short, it is opportunity that matters most—both for growth and for social and political stability."

The new perspective of seeing the regional economy as a "growth engine," by elected representatives means pursuing four institutional goals:

1. Increasing the number of market transactions which occur in the regional economy. It does not particularly matter what kinds of markets operate in the economy. It could be farmer's markets, flea markets, gold coin markets, capital markets, or labor markets. Market exchange increases the flow of market information by allowing direct face-to-face communication among regional residents. Face-to-face communication increases the level of trust among citizens and creates the conditions for knowledge creation and knowledge diffusion. Increasing market transactions means that elected representatives create a "knowledge-based economy."

2. Increasing the rate of new high technology ventures within the region. New technology ventures create new future markets for goods and services which do not currently exist. The new future markets create new income distribution networks which allow citizens to obtain wealth and prosperity, not trapped by the existing status quo of social class barriers.

3. Increasing the rate of profit reinvestment by new technology ventures in the region. The initial round of investment, in year 1, is important, but the economic growth occurs in the region in year 5, when the profits are reinvested back into the regional economy. Regional new ventures have a greater territorial loyalty and allegiance to the increasing the prosperity of the region, in contrast to

large corporations who have no loyalty or allegiance to citizen or national sovereignty.

4. Increased elected representative regional trade collaboration. The new growth perspective means that elected representatives begin seeing other metro regional leaders as collaborators, and not competitors in the dead-end game of industrial recruitment incentives. Increased trade agreements, based upon regional technology specialization, would conform to the benefits of international trade theory of an earlier era.

In the context of replacing Madison's Preamble with a new constitutional preamble, the promotion of the initial American factor endowment of individual creativity and initiative would be called creating a "commonwealth of independent producers."

In other words, the constitutional public purpose would not be a system of checks and balances between the ruling class natural aristocracy and common citizens.

The new entrepreneurial capitalist constitutional public purpose would aim at creating a society of equal rights for all and special privileges for none.

Chapter 8. Towards An Absolute National Divorce and The Creation of A New Constitution.

Politics in America changed, forever, after Obama's election in 2008, and after the beginning of the collaboration between globalist corporations and Marxist Democrats, which undermines the national sovereignty of the United States.

We have argued that the best solution to the irreconcilable conflict is an absolute national divorce, and allowing citizens in each state to vote on creating a new nation.

We have argued that the authentic founding of America was in 1776, not 1787.

We claim that the documents and philosophy of George Mason and Thomas Jefferson, as codified in the state sovereignty framework of the Articles of Confederation, are the essential historical guides that citizens can use to build a new constitution. (George Mason's America: The State Sovereignty Alternative to Madison's Centralized Ruling Class Aristocracy. Gabby Press, 2023.).

We ask:

If citizens in America, today, were provided the opportunity to follow Buchanan's rules for creating a new constitution, relying on Mason's individualist ideology, what would the market and social institutional structure of the new society look like?

We suspect that Buchanan's concept of creating constitutional rules would lead to an institutionally stable middle class social order, based upon voluntary citizen cooperation, which would not require the police state oppression of the Marxist two-tiered justice system.

A new constitution, today, with Mason's concept of individual liberty, placed within Buchanan's constitutional framework, and Schumpeter's entrepreneurial capitalist economy provides a pathway for American citizens out of the Marxist Democrat/global corporatist Leviathan.

Buchanan's constitution is based upon social class cooperation, not Madison's social class conflict, among individuals who are seeking to improve their own financial condition through free market exchange with other individuals.

As Buchanan points out, voluntary allegiance to the rule of law results from the realization that it is in one's best interest for his or her life's mission to be consistent with the public purpose of rules that citizens give to themselves.

Madison made a moral wager, proven a failure in history, that all citizens, rich and poor alike, would flourish under his constitutional rules because he assumed that ruling class elites would create and preserve the balance of power to achieve social stability between the two social classes.

We argue that natural rights conservatives, today, would opt out of Madison's defective system, if given the option of providing consent to continue under his rules, or else to leave the state of nature to start over, at 1776.

Madison's constitution devolved into an unelected, unaccountable tyranny that advocates globalism, not the sovereign national economic interest.

There are not two political parties that represent distinct social classes, as intended by Madison's British mixed government model.

Both political parties, for different reasons, promote globalization of the American economy, to the detriment of the sovereign national economic interest.

The ruling class in Washington operate for their own financial benefit, disconnected from any concept of the consent of the governed.

As Mason accurately predicted, on the last day of Madison's convention, in September of 1787,

"These gentlemen who will be elected senators, will fix themselves in the federalist town, and become citizens of that town more than of your state."

"This government will commence in a moderate aristocracy," Mason said.

He added,

"It is at present impossible to foresee whether it will, in its operation, produce a monarchy or a corrupt, oppressive aristocracy, it will most probably vitiate some years (233) between the two, and then terminate in the one or the other." (2020).

With the benefit of historical observation, we conclude that Madison's government ended on November 3, 2020, in a tyrannical unelected oppressive plutocracy.

The main idea, we propose, for a new constitution is to place individual liberty in the Preamble as the purpose of national government, in an entrepreneurial capitalist economy, in a decentralized state sovereignty framework.

Our conception of decentralized political power empowers state governments, and metropolitan regions to assume greater authority over the protection of citizen liberties and economic growth.

We advocate a national economic policy of economic sovereignty, based upon the concept of entrepreneurial capitalism.

We argue that a better form of government, than an oppressive plutocracy, is a constitutional democratic republic, which defines the mission of the national government as the protection and preservation of individual liberty.

The new Constitution of the Democratic Republic of American States must be ratified by the citizens in the states that choose to join the new democratic confederation.

We propose that state legislatures manage a citizen's constitutional referendum in each state that provides citizens with a choice of 3 constitutional options:

1. Allow the citizens of a state to vote to maintain its membership in the current U. S. constitutional framework, to be called the Former United States. [FUSA].
2. Allow the citizens to vote to join the Socialist States of America, in confederation with California and any other state, where the citizens vote to live under a socialist regime.
3. Allow the citizens to join the Democratic Republic of American States, the new natural rights republic.

We follow Buchanan's principles of creating rules for the constitution that he calls " the protective national state," which include:

- Rules on economic competition and prohibitions on monopoly or unfair and deceptive trade practices.

- Rules on fair access to loans and capital to start new ventures or expand existing business.
- Protection of open flows of information and knowledge for technology innovation.
- Protection of national sovereign technology innovation and intellectual property rights.
- Rules on the prohibition on special interest corporate lobbying and rule manipulation and conflict of interest of government agents and elected representatives to use the agencies of government to limit competition or direct the benefits of economic growth to their own social class.

In Buchanan's sequence of events in creating a new constitution, social and political institutions are created by elected representatives, after the constitution has been ratified by a vote of the citizens.

Many of the social, political, and financial institutions for an entrepreneurial capitalist economy do not yet exist.

As we pointed out earlier, the financial and market institutions that currently exist are oriented to the benefit of the ruling class.

In the area of social institutions, we advocate the creation of social networks in each metro region that function to bring citizens together for the purpose of exploring new entrepreneurial ventures.

We have advocated the implementation of a social network block chain to manage this new type of entrepreneurial new venture creation function. (Vass, Laurie Thomas, Gabby Press, Updating Schumpeter's Gales of Creative Destruction: Exploiting the Vulnerability of New World Order Corporate Globalism With Regional Blockchain Entrepreneurial Economic Growth. 2022.).

We explain in our book on Schumpeter;

"Based upon an analysis of the components of U. S. GDP, after the economic collapse of 2008, about 80% of all GDP was related to six service industrial sectors, [restaurants, travel, recreation], which employ about 70% of the U. S. workforce, [gig economy]…About 20% of U. S. GDP is related to the industrial sectors engaged in global trade, in the global corporate macrotechnology…We estimate that the new world order economic model benefits about 20% of the U. S. population, who get richer and richer from the operation of the global corporate model…We argue that the ultimate economic consequence of new world corporatism is world-wide economic collapse because there is insufficient knowledge creation and diffusion, outside of the corporate vertical value chains."

That new knowledge creation must result in hundreds of thousands of new technology ventures, every year.

About 65% of all new technology ventures die in the first 5 years.

The average employment in a new technology venture in the first year is 4 jobs. All new net job creation in the U. S. is related to the creation of very small technology firms.

At age 6, each new venture requires the injection of new capital to survive and grow. If the new firm can survive to age 9, the rate of job growth doubles, from around 5 employees to 10 employees.

At age 12, the rate of job growth of a technology new venture is exponential.

In the area of capital market institutions, we have advocated supplementing the existing venture capital business model with a regional capital market infrastructure, whose goal is new venture creation in the nine high technology industrial clusters.

Part of the barrier to regional new venture creation is the absence of a capital market institutional infrastructure. The existing venture capital networks, and angel funding forums, are not adequate for the level of new venture creation required to stimulate regional economic growth.

Most private securities for new technology ventures are bought and sold by venture capitalist firms, who have the market power to enforce the exit because of the terms and conditions that they insert into the offering documents.

Part of the issue is that the investment capital required by small manufacturing firms and startups to support innovation is so small that it is not attractive to the VCs.

And, part of the issue is that the preferred quick VC exit strategy does not contribute to long-term economic growth at the regional level.

In other words, there is a financial conflict of interest between the short-term financial interests of the venture capitalist community and the long-term goals of regional self-sustaining economic growth.

More venture capital, as it is currently deployed, will not solve the capital equity gap for regional innovation. (Vass Laurie Thomas, Will More Venture Capital Spur Regional Innovation? SSRN, 2008.).

A new regional capital market infrastructure must be built in each region that targets investments into the region's industrial value chains.

The new capital market infrastructure must address the small amounts of capital required at the front end of the innovation pipeline, the additional small amount of capital required by the venture in year 6, and the best economic strategy that promotes economic growth at the back end of the pipeline.

The model of new venture economic growth would look like the corporate history of SAS Institute, of Raleigh, N. C., which was started by three N. C. State University students, on the campus, in the late 1960s.

SAS grew from $10 million in revenues in 1980 to $1.1 billion by 2000. The company currently employs over 12,000 people, world-wide.

SAS is currently the largest privately-held company in the world, which argues for the idea that the best goal of regional economic development is to grow small technology companies into profitable big companies, and not follow the quick-exit strategy of the venture capitalist model.

Internet based local crowd funding will tend to organize local social business networks into a coherent capital market that targets investments to the region's most promising technological innovations.

We predict that the local and metro social business networks on the internet will eventually become the local equivalent of capital market exchanges, like the New York Stock Exchange.

The regional capital market exchange infrastructure will contain the following components:

- FINRA Broker Dealers, whose sales staff conduct buying and selling of both private and public securities.
- FDIC commercial bankers, who extend loans and credit, when the small company has sufficient collateral. In the case of Reg D 506c, the capital obtained through the offering will act as collateral for the commercial banks to extend credit.
- Registered investment advisors, who provide professional guidance to technology CEOs on how to issue the securities and qualify the securities for trading in the secondary market.
- Institutional merger and acquisition bankers, who act as market intermediaries for combining companies into larger entities.
- Asst-based lenders and commercial finance companies who provide inventory financing and factoring.
- Pooled investment funds and private equity funds that raise larger amounts of capital, and use the capital much like venture capitalists do when they raise a large VC fund.
- Venture capital firms and angel capital partnerships.
- Back-office stock custodians and transfer agents who handle the administration of issuing securities.

The most important function of new venture creation in regional capital markets, however, is not the initial investment in a single firm.

The most important economic growth function is that the regional markets will provide a pathway for profits from the exit events to be re-invested in the regional innovation economy, in a type of Bayesian economic success model.

The regional black chain networks, based upon internet technologies, provide the mechanism for this re-investment of capital from one generation of innovation to the next, unleashing a torrent of capital investment and an explosion of job creation.

Moving American innovation technology and R&D to India and China is perfectly legal, under Madison's ruling class economic system because there is no constitutional telos, or end goal, that states that the ruling class improve the the welfare of common citizens.

Trading away America's ability to radically innovate undermines the basic promise, in a natural rights republic, that citizens make to each other not to destroy America's heritage in order to gain personal financial advantage.

Once traded away, America's initial factor endowment of radical technology innovation was permanently disabled. American citizens have no process of grievance, against the corporate elite and socialists who colluded on trade policies, in 1992.

Among the many barriers to implementing this economic growth strategy, in addition to the non-existent regional capital market framework, is that the organizational and institutional structure to support knowledge creation and diffusion is non-existent.

The current, existing technology innovation model is a closed-proprietary, network of codified knowledge diffusion, tightly controlled by large corporations, in collaboration with university tech-transfer agents, who benefit financially from this symbiotic relationship. (Vass, Laurie Thomas, Unchallenged Assumptions About Innovation Meet Shibboleths of University Tech Transfer, SSRN. 2020.).

This technology innovation model of global corporations and university tech transfer agents facilitates global corporate value chains, to the economic detriment of U. S. economic sovereignty. (Vass, Laurie Thomas, The Unintended Consequences of American University Tech Transfer: Does it Facilitate the Offshoring of American R&D? SSRN. 2009.).

We argue that the same block chain model for regional capital markets performs double duty as the regional tacit technology knowledge creation and diffusion networks, required to re-establish the American initial factor endowment of new venture creation in each metro region.

The entire regional economic development strategy is based upon allowing individual citizens to seek wealth and prosperity.

The achievement of that goal depends upon a certain type of constitutional configuration of rules and the subsequent creation of social, political, and market institutions, after the constitution has been ratified by a vote of the citizens.

The function of government at the state and regional metro level consists of implementing and administering institutions that facilitate economic growth through new venture creation.

The function of the national government is to create the protective state, which protects individual liberty, as advocated by Buchanan.

We argued in America's Final Revolution, that the first revolution, of 1776, left the business of liberty unfinished, and that a final revolution is required to reclaim the ideals of liberty. (Vass, Laurie Thomas, America's Final Revolution: Reconstructing Jefferson's American Dream of An Entrepreneurial Capitalist Society. Gabby Press. 2022.).

We have offered our thoughts on the principles of government that can form the basis of the decentralized state sovereignty framework for the new constitution of The Democratic Republic of American States.

Our argument in this book is that a new constitution with Mason's concept of individual liberty, placed within Buchanan's constitutional framework, and Schumpeter's entrepreneurial capitalist economy provides a pathway for American citizens back to the original intent of George Mason and Thomas Jefferson, in their respective documents of 1776.

The synthesis of thought of Mason, Buchanan, and Schumpeter provides the starting point of the national debate over what form of government replaces Madison's flawed constitution.

As a starting point of discussion and debate about the new constitution, we offer these principles:

Preamble:

We, the citizens of the states of The Democratic Republic of American States, establish this constitutional contract between our respective states and the National Government.

"We solemnly swear and affirm that we establish this contract to preserve and protect the natural and civil rights of citizens in each state, and to protect and defend the sovereignty of each state and the nation, from foreign and domestic threats."

Citizen Bill of Rights of the Democratic Republic of American States.

In creating this constitution, we affirm and swear that all citizens in each of the respective States are guaranteed equal rights for all, and special privileges for none.

Among these rights are:

1. That all citizens have a natural right to worship and exercise their own religion and that the National Government is prohibited from making and enforcing any law respecting the establishment of an official national religion and compelling citizens to worship a national religion.
2. The National Government shall be prohibited from making or enforcing any law that restricts the natural right of a citizen's freedom of speech and freedom of conscience.
3. The National Government is prohibited from making or enforcing any law which restricts the right of citizens to peaceably assemble, and to petition the National Government for a redress of grievances.
4. That all citizens have a natural right to truthful and honest statements from government agents and from elected representatives, and that it is the duty of the free press to report the truth.
5. That all citizens in the respective states have a natural right to own and use weapons, and that the

National Government, nor any state, shall make no laws which abridge the right of law-abiding citizens from owning, keeping and bearing weapons.
6. The National Government is prohibited from using agents of government or national resources to conduct searches and seizures of private citizen documents, or property, and that the possessions and documents obtained from illegal searches and seizures are inadmissible in any national court.
7. No citizen in any state shall be seized or imprisoned, or stripped of his rights or of his property or possessions, or outlawed or exiled, or deprived of his standing in any other way, nor shall agents of the government proceed with force against him, or send others to do so, except by the lawful judgment of a true bill of indictment by a majority vote of a grand jury of 18 citizens, or by the rules of judicial civil procedure of the National Government.
8. No warrants or judicial orders in any criminal investigation shall be issued by a national court, except upon probable cause, determined in a judicial hearing, supported by an oath or affirmation of the government agent describing the specific items or locations to be searched and a judicial description of the crime being investigated.
9. No person shall be held to answer for a capital, or otherwise infamous crime, unless on a presentment or indictment of a majority vote of a Grand Jury of

18 citizens who conduct an inquiry into the legitimacy of the government's allegation of a national crime.
10. No citizen shall be subject for the same offence or to be twice put in jeopardy of life or limb; nor shall be compelled in any criminal case to be a witness against himself.
11. The National Government, and every State government, are prohibited from making or enforcing any law which shall abridge the privileges or immunities of citizens of the States; nor shall any State deprive any natural human person of life, liberty, or property, without due process of law; nor deny to any person within its jurisdiction the equal protection of the laws.
12. No citizen shall be deprived of life, liberty, or property, without due process of law; nor shall private property be taken for public use, without just compensation, determined by a majority vote of a Grand Jury of 18 citizens.
13. That all citizens are due the equal application of justice and that no citizen, elected representative, or agent of government, is entitled to special or unequal treatment of the application of the law.
14. That all citizens in any criminal or civil proceeding, are presumed innocent until proven guilty in a trial of due process, by a jury of 12 of their peers.

15. In all criminal prosecutions, the accused shall enjoy the right to a speedy and public trial, within 6 months of indictment, by an impartial jury of the State and district wherein the crime shall have been committed, which district shall have been previously ascertained by law, and to be informed of the nature and cause of the accusation; to be confronted with the witnesses against him; to have compulsory process for obtaining witnesses in his favor, and to have the assistance of counsel for his defense.
16. The right of trial by jury shall be preserved, and no fact tried by a jury, shall be otherwise re-examined in any Court of the States, than according to the rules of the common law then obtaining in the national judiciary.
17. Excessive bail shall not be required, nor excessive fines imposed, nor cruel and unusual punishments inflicted, nor imprisonment for longer than 5 days, in the absence of specific charges and allegation of crime.
18. That citizens have a civil right of action against elected representatives or agents of the National Government, for violation of these natural rights, upon a presentation of a motion of grievance to a Grand Jury of 18 citizens, who shall hear the case and determine the outcome and set the penalties for the violation by a majority vote.

19. The a citizens Grand Jury in any State retains the right of initiating a citizen initiative on legislative proposals or access to government documents, by a petition to the House of Representatives, which must respond to the petition within 30 days of receipt.
20. The right of citizens of the States to vote, hold elected office, or deliberate in public debates, shall not be denied or abridged by the National Government or by any State on account of race, color of skin, biological sex, or religious beliefs.
21. The right of a citizen to vote in all elections is an inviolable inalienable natural right, and is constitutionally protected, in both the citizen's freedom to vote and in the legitimate count of the vote, in all local, state, and national elections and referendums, by Federal and State law enforcement agents.

Bibliography: A Civil Dissolution.

Alinsky, Saul, Rules for Radicals: A Pragmatic Primer for Realistic Radicals, 1971.

Anton, Michael, The Stakes: America at the Point of No Return, 2020.

Appleby, Joyce, Capitalism and a New Social Order: The Republican Vision of the 1790s, 1984.

Arendt, Hannah, The Origins of Totalitarianism, 1951.

Autor, David H., Dorn, David, Hanson, Gordon H., The China Syndrome: Local Labor Market Effects of Import Competition In The United States, , NBER Working Paper 18054, 2012.

Autor, David H., and Dorn, David, The Growth of Low-Skill Service Jobs and the Polarization of the US Labor Market, American Economic Review, 2013.

Baker, Kevin, It's Time for a Bluexit A declaration of independence from Trump's America. New Republic, March 9, 2017.

Baumol, William J., Litan, Robert E., and Schramm, Carl J., Good Capitalism, Bad Capitalism, and the Economics of Growth and Prosperity, 2007.

Beard, Charles, An Economic Interpretation of the Constitution of the United States, 1925.

Beauchamp, Zack, The Constitution Was Not Built For This, Vox, 2023.

Blackstone, William, Commentaries on the Laws of England, 1765.

Boettke, Peter J. and Coyne, Christopher J., Methodological Individualism, Spontaneous Order and the Research Program of the Workshop in Political Theory and Policy Analysis, George Mason University, Department of Economics, 2004.

Brown, Richard D., Revolutionary Politics in Massachusetts: The Boston Committee of Correspondence and the Towns, 1772-1774, 1976.

Buchanan, James M., The Limits of Liberty: Between Anarchy and Leviathan, 1975.

Buchanan, James M., Logical Foundations of Constitutional Liberty, 1999.

Buchanan, James M., "Rent Seeking and Profit Seeking," in, James M. Buchanan, Robert Tollison, and Gordon Tullock (eds). Toward a Theory of the Rent-Seeking Society, 1980.

Buchanan, James M., The Theory of Public Choice, 1972.

Buchanan, James M., and Brennan, Geoffrey, Reason of Rules, Cambridge University Press, 1985.

Buchanan, James M., and Congleton, Roger D., Politics By Principle, Not Interest, , 1998.

Burke, Edmund, Thoughts on the Present Discontents, 1770.

Cash, W. J., The Mind of the South, 1941.

Christensen, Clayton, The Innovator's Dilemma, 1997.

Cialdini Robert B., Influence: Science and Practice, 2001.

Codevilla, Angelo M., America's Ruling Class And the Perils of Revolution, 2010.

Cornell, Saul, The Other Founders, 1999.

Coyne, Christopher J., and Hall, Abigail R., Cronyism: Necessary for the Minimal, Protective State, GMU Working Paper in Economics No. 18-26 SSRN. July 2018

DeVega, Chauncey, Yes, Trump will leave office but his seditious secession Salon. 2020.

Díez Federico J., Leigh, Daniel and Tambunlertchai, Suchanan, IMF Working Paper, WP/18/137 2018.

De Soto, Hernando, The Mystery of Capital, 2003.

De Soto, Hernando, The Other Path: The Economic Answer to Terrorism, 2002.

DeTocqueville, Alexis, Democracy in America, 1835.

Dicey, A.V., The Law of the Constitution, 1885.

Domhoff, William, Who Rules America, Power, Politics, & Social Change. 2021

Douglas, Elisha, P., Rebels and Democrats, 1955.

Duffner, Stephan et al., Trust and Success in Venture Capital Financing—an Empirical Analysis with German Survey Data, 2009.

Farber, Daniel, and Sherry, Suzanna, Beyond All Reason: The Radical Assault on Truth in American Law, 1997.

Faris David, It's Time to Fight Dirty: How Democrats Can Build a Lasting Majority in American Politics, 2018.

Farrand, Max, The Records of the Federal Convention of 1787, 3vols., 1911.

Florida, Richard, The Distinct Personality of Entrepreneurial Cities, Bloomberg, 2015.

French, David, Divided We Fall: America's Secession Threat and How to Restore Our Nation, 2020.

Gereffi, Gary, and Fernandez-Stark, Karina, Global Value Chain Analysis: A Primer, Second Edition. The Duke Center on Globalization, Governance & Competitiveness, 2016.

Goodwyn, Lawrence, The Populist Moment: A Short History of the Agrarian Revolt in America, 1978.

Halpin, John, The Politics of Definition, Prospect, 2006.

Haltiwanger, John C., Jarmin, Ron S., Miranda, Javier, Who Creates Jobs? Small Vs. Large Vs. Young, NBER Working Paper 16300, 2010.

Hathaway, Ian, Tech Starts: High-Technology Business Formation and Job Creation in the United States, Kauffman Foundation Research Series, 2013.

Hayek, Friedrich A., Constitution of Liberty, 1978.

Hayek, Fredrich, A., The Road to Serfdom, Routledge, 1944.

Heer, Jeet, The Republican Party, Not Trump, Is the Real Threat to American Democracy, The New Republic, 2018.

Hobbes, Thomas, The Leviathan, first published, 1651.

Hoffert, Robert, A Politics of Tensions: The Articles of Confederation and American Political Ideas, 1992.

Horwitz, Robert, The Moral Foundations of the American Republic, 1986.

Hyland, William G., George Mason: The Founding Father Who Gave Us The Bill of Rights, 2019.

Jaffa, Harry, Crisis of the House Divided: An Interpretation of the Issues in the Lincoln-Douglas Debates, 1959.

Jensen, Merrill, The Articles of Confederation, 1970.

Jowett, Garth, Propaganda and Persuasion. 1992.

Kaminsky John, and Leffler, Richard, ed., Federalists and Antifederalists: The Debate Over the Ratification of the Constitution, 1998.

Kant, Immanuel, The Metaphysics of Morals, Translated by Mary J. Gregor. 1991. first published 1797.

Kreitner, Richard, Break It Up: Secession, Division, and the Secret History of America's Imperfect Union, 2020.

Laila, Cristina, Domestic Violent Extremists, Gateway Pundit, August 16, 2022.

Lake, Eli, Bloomberg News, 2021.

Levin, Mark, The Liberty Amendments: Restoring the American Republic, 2013.

Levy, Jacob T., Beyond Publius: Montesquieu, Liberal Republicanism and the Small-Republic Thesis, JSTOR, 2006.

Livingston, James, Origins of the Federal Reserve System, Money, Class, and Corporate Capitalism, 1890-1913., 1986.

Locke, John, Second Treatise on Government, 2016, first published 1689.

Loecker, Jan, Eeckhout, De Jan, The Rise of Market Power and The Macroeconomic Implications, NBER Working Paper 23687, 2017.

Mackie, J. L , Ethics: Inventing Right and Wrong, 1977.

Macpherson, C. B., The Political Theory of Possessive Individualism, 2010.

McDonald. Forrest, A Constitutional History of the United States. 1982.

Milgram, Stanley, Obedience to Authority: An Experimental View, 1974.

Mokyr, Joel, The Lever of Riches: Technological Creativity and Economic Progress, 1990.

Morton, Joseph C., The Constitutional Convention of 1787: A Biographical Dictionary, 2006.

Munger, Michael and Villarreal-Diaz Mario, The Road to Crony Capitalism, The Independent Review, Winter 2019.

Paine, Thomas, Common Sense, 2016, first published 1775.

Paxton, Robert, Vichy France: Old Guard and New Order, 2015.

Rakove, Jack N., Declaring Rights: A Brief History with Documents, 1998.

Rawls, John A., Theory of Justice, 1971.

Reiman, Jeffrey, Justice and Modern Moral Philosophy, 1990.

Robinson, Emerald, The Biden Regime Goes Rogue, Substack, 2022.

Romer, Paul, What Drives Economic Growth, 2018.

Rutland, Robert A., George Mason: Reluctant Statesman, 1961.

Saviotti, Piero, Technological Evolution, Variety and the Economy, 1996.

Scheiber, Noam, New Republic May 30, 2007.

Schumpeter, Joseph A., Capitalism, Socialism and Democracy, 1942.

Siemers, David J., The Antifederalists: Men of Great Faith and Forbearance, 2003.

Sisson, Dan, The American Revolution of 1800, 2014.

Slonim, Shlomo, Framers' Construction/Beardian Deconstruction, Essays on the Constitutional Design of 1787, 2001.

Smith, Adam, An Inquiry Into the Nature and Causes of the Wealth of Nations, 1776.

Sobel, Russell and Graefe-Anderson, Rachel, The Relationship between Political Connections and the Financial Performance of Industries & Firms, Mercatus Working Paper, SSRN, 2018.

Spulber, Daniel F., Competition Policy and the Incentive to Innovate: The Dynamic Effects of Microsoft v. Commission, Yale Journal on Regulation, Volume 25, Number 2, Summer 2008.

Sundance, A Specific Type of Continuity, The Last Refuge, July 21, 2023.

Sunstein, Cass, Democracy and the Problem of Free Speech, 1995.

Sunstein, Cass, Designing Democracy: What Constitutions Do, 2002.

Suriano, Jessica, Should the United States Stay United?, The Nation, 2020.

Tarter, Brent, George Mason and the Conservation of Liberty, The Virginia Magazine of History and Biography, July 1991.

Thompson, C. Bradley, Why Marxism—Evil Laid Bare, 2012.

Thompson, C. Bradley, America's Revolutionary Mind: A Moral History of the American Revolution and the Declaration that Defined It, 2019.

Thompson, Derek, Who Are Donald Trump's Supporters, Really? The Atlantic, 2016.

Tuck, Richard, Natural Rights Theories: Their Origin and Development, 1981.

Ufuk, Akcigit, et al., Innovation and Trade Policy in a Globalized World, NBER Working Paper 24543, 2018.

Van Alstyne, William, A Critical Guide to Marbury v. Madison, Duke Law Journal, 1969.

Vass, Laurie Thomas, America's Final Revolution: Reconstructing Jefferson's American Dream of An Entrepreneurial Capitalist Society. Gabby Press. 2022..

Vass, Laurie Thomas, Equal Rights For All. Special Privileges for None. Re-Examining the Agrarian Arguments Against A Centralized American Government, Gabby Press. 2017.

Vass, Laurie Thomas, George Mason's America: The State Sovereignty Alternative to Madison's Centralized American Ruling Class Aristocracy, Gabby Press. 2023.

Vass, Laurie Thomas, Predicting Technology, Gabby Press, 2007.

Vass, Laurie Thomas, The American Rule of Law and the Collapse of the American Economy, SSRN, The Private Capital Market Working Paper No. 08-07-04. 2008.

Vass, Laurie Thomas, The Economic and Political Consequences of European-Style Innovation Policy, SSRN, The Private Capital Market Working Paper No. 2008-04-04. 2008.

Vass, Laurie Thomas, The Restoration of the Natural Rights Republic, Gabby Press, 2017, first published 2008.

Vass, Laurie Thomas, The Unintended Consequences of American University Tech Transfer: Does it Facilitate the Offshoring of American R&D? SSRN. 2009.

Vass, Laurie Thomas, Unchallenged Assumptions About Innovation Meet Shibboleths of University Tech Transfer, SSRN. 2020.

Vass, Laurie Thomas, Updating Schumpeter's Gales of Creative Destruction: Exploiting the Vulnerability of New World Order Corporate Globalism With Regional Blockchain Entrepreneurial Economic Growth. Gabby Press, 2022.

Vass, Laurie Thomas, Will More Venture Capital Spur Regional Innovation? SSRN, 2008.

Vaughn, Karen, John Locke and the Labor Theory of Value, Journal of Libertarian Studies, 1978.

Vaughn, Karen, John Locke: Economist and Social Scientist, 2012.

Wilentz Sean, No Property in Man: Slavery and Antislavery at the Nation's Founding, 2018.

Wilenz, Sean, The Rise of American Democracy: Jefferson to Lincoln, 2006.

Winkler Adam, Corporations Are People' Is Built on an Incredible 19th-Century Lie: How a farcical series of events in the 1880s produced an enduring and controversial legal precedent, The Atlantic, 2018.

Wright, Robin, Is America a Myth?, New Yorker, September 2020.

Wood Gordon, S., The Creation of the American Republic, 1776 – 1787, 1969.

Zimbardo, Phil. Understanding Mind Control, New York: HarperCollins, 1993.

Zinn, Howard, People's History of the United States, 2016.

Zuckert, Michael, The Natural Rights Republic: Studies In The Foundation of The American Political Tradition, 1996.

Zywicki, Todd J., Rent-Seeking, Crony Capitalism, and the Crony Constitution, George Mason Legal Studies Research Paper No. LS 15-08; George Mason Law & Economics Research Paper No. 15-26. August 26, 2015.

www.ingramcontent.com/pod-product-compliance
Lightning Source LLC
LaVergne TN
LVHW021957060526
838201LV00048B/1599